Education for Family Life

Education for Family Life

# Education for Family Life
*some new policies for child care*

Richard C. Whitfield

**HODDER AND STOUGHTON**
LONDON   SYDNEY   AUCKLAND   TORONTO

The poem on page 135 is by Richard C. Whitfield.
© 1979 R C Whitfield

Whitfield, Richard Charles
    Education for family life.
    1. Children – Management – Study and teaching
    (Secondary)
    I. Title
    649' .1' 0712        HQ755.7

    ISBN 0 340 25524 2

First published 1980
Copyright © 1980 Richard C. Whitfield and National Children's Home

Printed and bound in Great Britain for
Hodder and Stoughton Educational,
a division of Hodder and Stoughton Ltd,
Mill Road, Dunton Green, Sevenoaks, Kent,
by Biddles of Guildford.

Phototypesetting by Swiftpages Limited, Liverpool

# Contents

v

# Figures

# Tables

# Preface

Those of us who are parents know how difficult it can be to execute that role effectively and yet lead an authentic life of our own. For those who are to become parents, many challenges lie ahead for which support from outside the nuclear family is frequently essential. For those who have no effective parents, and are in full-time residential care, the dedication of staff can frequently compensate but can rarely be a viable substitute for a stable family life.

The stimulus to write this book arose from the kind invitation I received from the Reverend Gordon Barritt, Principal of the National Children's Home (NCH), to deliver the 1979 Convocation Lecture at the Hayes Conference Centre, Swanwick, Derbyshire on 9 June 1979. Gordon knew of my concern for the concept of 'Preparation for Parenthood', but gave me freedom to develop a theme within the broad area of child care as a part of the NCH's efforts in the 1979 International Year of the Child.

*Education for Family Life* is thus centrally concerned with aspects of parent preparation, but I have deliberately widened the canvas to set my educational suggestions in their broader context. It is to be hoped, therefore, in so far as there is prescription in my account, that the suggestions are adequately based upon a legitimate interpretation of such research findings as are available, though they are of course unavoidably related to my own value position, for which I hope I have given adequate justification as the text develops. I also hope that the text is relatively free of the worst excesses of academic jargon, so that much of it can be read without too much difficulty by a wide audience. With that aim in mind, I have deliberately avoided giving too many footnotes and detailed references, though a structured bibliography is provided (see pages 158-9 and bibliographical references following the various chapters).

As a teacher and educationist, rather than social worker, sociologist or psychologist, I focus my attention specifically towards *prevention* of family care problems through teaching and educational intervention, rather than on their correction through counselling and the informal or statutorily extended support of families already identified as crisis cases. This emphasis is, however, not intended to polarise relationships between prevention and remediation, for *both* are crucial elements in any overall policy of social concern. My intention has been to look at the conditions, the pre-requisites, and the necessities upon which effective care within families of all its members is contingent; it will be for others with more specialist competencies to put the substantive and administrative flesh upon this framework. But it must be noted that there are many interesting innovations which need recognising and encouraging within a more cohesive framework of care, some of which are listed in Appendices 2 and 3 (pages 138–57).

My approach has not been from a narrow, restrictive, nor indeed romanticised view of the family, though the task of creating some degree of scholarly yet practical order within the field of family care, which has so many diverse professional and academic facets, is not easy. Perhaps for that reason the area has been insufficiently written about in recent years with inter-related objectives in view. In many ways the task which I set myself was too extensive, and this volume should be considered as no more than a step forward in the field. If it causes constructive discussions between educators, health specialists, social workers and the communities which they serve for the ultimate well-being of both children and parents, then I shall be pleased. However, as Chapter 6 makes clear, I will not be satisfied until we have, through central and local government initiatives, a more specific range of policies which transcend political affiliation and are designed to promote lifelong family care. Only with such policies, drafted on a long-term basis, will we be in a position to utilise more effectively the potentials of the social, educational and health care facilities in which the community now makes such massive investments.

In choosing to compile a text concerning educational and social policy, it is difficult for any author to step outside his own biography. In this particular case, it seemed unlikely from the start that an 'antiseptic' or purely academic work would result. In parts I have deliberately stated a personal position extrapolated from limited evidence and understanding; but most of the text is grounded in a realistic contemporary assessment of the needs of children and those who have responsibility for their care. In the epilogue, in particular, I have tried to indicate something of how a radical Christian perspective has illuminated my understanding. Emphatically, however, my case does not depend upon Christian faith; that faith simply gives me personally an 'eternal' purpose to action and 'answers' the paradox of why anyone should care for others to the point of self-denial, which is what any form of effective child care at times inevitably involves.

In preparing a book of this kind there are many who have made both indirect and direct contributions to the development of my ideas. Other writers are acknowledged in the text, but here I must mention specifically Sir Richard Acland, through whose persistence we set up the informal 'Preparation for Parenthood Group' (see Appendix 1, pages 136–7), Dorothy Baldwin (author and teacher) and my Senior Research colleague in this field, Martin Vegoda, who have both read the bulk of the text in draft and made valuable and frank comments. Other Aston Departmental colleagues, notably Christine Atkinson, John Bradshaw, Peter Coxhead, Richard Nelson-Jones and Geoffrey Walford, made me think twice about aspects of my position as I deliberately ran the gauntlet of their probings from their disciplines of philosophy, psychology, sociology and research methods; I suspect that I am unlikely to have met all their objections in my synthesis. Patricia Hunt and Neil Grant kindly assisted me with surveys of the diverse literature in the summer of 1978, and were able to confirm the lack of coherence of both the academic background and the related social and educational policies appropriate to the field. Retired HM Staff Inspector for schools and Senior Research Associate at Aston, 'Sam' Comber assisted me in the closing stages of manuscript preparation in simplifying some of the language, and also provided a few useful background notes in the spring of 1979; at this point I found the publication of Joseph Featherstone's paper 'Family Matters' (see references to Chapter 6), giving a perspective from the USA, particularly timely and of influence in the last two chapters. Sister Margaret Hobbs, former superintendent of the NCH Ladywood Family Centre in Birmingham, kindly distilled for me something of her often agonising professional experience of child care and families in need, and I am grateful to Helen Shute for helping with some of the proof-reading and for compiling the index.

Things learned, perhaps unconsciously, from my own parents and from my own family and work settings have undoubtedly been of influence. My wife Shirley and our four children (Mark 14, Philip 13, Michael 9, and Katherine 2) have borne some of the pain of creation and absence from interaction which authorship demands, particularly in a field in which, if we are honest, there are no real experts; they know first hand the significant gap between father's good intentions and his personal practice. Finally, I acknowledge the loyal, efficient and cheerful support of my secretary, Lynne Harris, who typed from my messy drafts and, assisted by Wendy Bayliss, kept me on course in the preparation of this manuscript for the publisher. Notwithstanding my gratitude to all these people, I alone take responsibility for the form of the final manuscript.

*Birmingham,*                                                          *Richard Whitfield*
*March 1980*

NOTE

The National Children's Home Convocation Lectures have been published annually since 1946 and many are still available in book form. If you are interested, please write to the National Children's Home, 85 Highbury Park, London, N5 1UD.

*The United Nations Declaration of the Rights of the Child (1959)*

The child shall enjoy special protection, and shall be
given opportunities and facilities, by law and by
other means, to enable him to develop physically,
mentally, morally, spiritually and socially in a
healthy and normal manner and in conditions of freedom
and dignity.

*Principle 2*

The child, for the full and harmonious development of
his personality, needs love and understanding. He
shall, wherever possible, grow up in the care and
under the responsibility of his parents, and in any
case in an atmosphere of affection and of moral and
material security; a child of tender years shall not,
save in exceptional circumstances, be separated from
his mother.

*Principle 6*

| Introduction

We live in a world of known crises rather than that of the relative ignorance of our forbears. Scientific discovery, education and mass communications inform us of impending world overpopulation, famine, resource shortage, environmental degradation, nuclear abuse and a range of technologies on the brink of being out of control in terms of serving the descendants of their creators. Yet we remain largely blind to reality, or find it so unpalatable that we let life take its course through the operation of market forces and the fumbling inertia of our political institutions. On our doorsteps, or, more correctly, by our firesides, there is a different yet seemingly growing crisis in the here and now which affects the quality of life for us today. The elemental building blocks of our social order—ordinary families—are under increasing stress as a result of changing ethics and economics, as well as developments in health, education and welfare provision. It is a pertinent question to ask whether our society values less than it once did the activities of being a parent, in terms of providing, within the family setting, consistent understanding and loving care for children during their formative years. And it is a truism that it is difficult to maintain high professional and ethical standards within activities whose worth is not consistently accepted by and celebrated within a community.

Consider these snapshots of today's reality.

* Gary, a toddler of three, is dragged along by the hand in the supermarket, falls over a pile of produce and begins to cry. His distraught mother yanks him to his feet, shouts at him, and slaps him, causing the child to cry even more.

* Susan is sixteen and has regularly played truant. Her parents, and father in particular, have had high career expectations for her, and have totally disapproved of her relationship with an older boy. The

1

local social services department has had to find her a place in a self-catering hostel for young women.

* Stephen at five can hardly talk because he has watched TV for five hours a day since he was a toddler, and his parents do not speak to him.

* At 21, Yvonne, a single girl, has had three children and an aborted pregnancy, and is now pregnant again. A heavy smoker, she weighs only five stones, and hospital staff suspect non-accidental injury to her youngest child.

* Ted looks after seven-months-old Karen while his wife is out at work. Karen pulls the teat off her bottle, the milk spills in her crib; she is spanked by her father, who remarks to a neighbour, 'She's been asking for that all day.'

* Tired of washing urine-soiled bedlinen, Hazel refuses to give Peter, aged four, anything to drink after his one cup of tea at breakfast.

* Jennifer, so far an only child, has always at home been given exactly what she wants, just when she wants it. Now at six she has severe problems of school phobia.

* Tony meets his new girlfriend in the pub each day after work because he cannot stand the noise of his three under-fives and his crabby wife at home.

In such ways some children are harmed daily because their parents either stumbled almost unconsciously into parenthood, or because, in response to complex social pressures, they feel that they have no alternative but to express resentment towards their children. Apparently overcome by responsibilities which they had not anticipated, and do not know how to tackle, often feeling isolated from opportunities for their own further development and personal fulfilment, they vent their frustrations directly or indirectly on their offspring. Some repeat, through an apparent lack of alternative models, the harsh treatment which they suffered two decades previously from their own parents. Others effectively copy their parents without questioning whether their own and their children's needs might differ.

And so the suffering mounts, for ignorance can compound resentment, and numbers of parents have a severely limited understanding of what might be reasonably expected of their children at different stages of their development. Many have little idea of relatively simple parental skills which they might employ to the benefit of their youngsters, and which could reduce the stress they feel. Most children in our society eventually become parents, yet traditionally we have offered little statutory experience and training to help them execute that role, which we naively assume to be instinctive or simply copied from others. The shrunken nuclear family (two children compared with about five a century ago), and the widespread disintegration of the effective extended family, along with other trends considered in Chapter 4, now make specific and positive educational intervention all the more essential.

This is not to imply that in the past the picture of child care has been a rosy one. Far from it, for such work as has been executed on the history of western childhood indicates that the earlier the historical period, the lower the level of child care and the more likely children were to be killed, beaten, terrorised, abandoned, or sexually abused. But scholarly findings, particularly in medicine, psychology, anthropology and sociology, now set new benchmarks for the morality and efficacy of child care practice, to which any really humane society cannot but fail to respond.

In the pages which follow, the need for preventive policies for effective family care will be charted, and an outline of their substance will be presented, the intention being to promote the well-being and growth to a fuller potential of both children and parents. Former President of the USA Henry Hoover once said: 'The attitude of nations towards child welfare will soon become the test of civilisation.'

The logic of the thesis to be developed is briefly as follows:

(a) There is in our society today significant underfunctioning among children and those who care for them. This underfunctioning is manifested in terms of degrees of insecurity and emotional stress, and the restricted developmment of the potentially rich range of human skills, intellectual abilities, attitudes and values within the distinctive modes of human consciousness and forms of understanding which enable persons to make sense of their experience.

(b) While underfunctioning is an inherent part of the human condition, at least some of it is preventable.

(c) Human underfunctioning is in part related to the way people treat each other in the diversity of social contexts. Some of the suffering and inhibited or retarded development among children is related to the nature of adult care and behaviour which they experience.

(d) Deficits and insensitivities in caring for children by adults are, at least partially, both remediable and preventable by educational measures which foster relevant knowledge and understanding, and develop appropriate skills and abilities derived from contemporary child care theory and practice.

(e) Preventive educational initiatives are however unlikely to have widespread impact upon child care unless they are accompanied by complementary modifications to a range of social policies which affect the total welfare of children and the adults who care for them. Furthermore, appropriate educational initiatives require cooperation among the diverse professional groups which impinge upon child welfare, along with their intention to build up individual capacities for self-help.

The realistic assumption is made that the vast majority of children will be reared for the forseeable future within a relatively small group of people, that is a family of the size now regarded as common in the Western world. Hence the title of the text includes the term 'family' specifically, although, as will be seen in Chapter 3, this is defined neither narrowly nor exclusively.

# CHAPTER 2

# Origins of Educational Achievement

Few people today question the desirability of children attending school. During the last 150 years a national system of education has become recognised as an essential attribute of any modern state. The education budget absorbs a major part of most national expenditure. Equal educational opportunity for all, whatever that may mean in practice, is a social justice objective of many social reform programmes. The extension of the compulsory period of schooling and an increasing proportion of young people going on to further and higher education are regarded as marks of social progress. But what are the outcomes of these formal educational processes, and how do the other major factors which impinge on pupils' and students' lives relate to and interact with them?

Superficially, a discussion of educational achievement might seem a curious topic to include in a text of this kind, but that is where this author's pilgrimage began with regard to issues of child care and parenthood almost a decade ago. Trained by means of a rigorous, specialised scientific curriculum from the age of sixteen, leavened only with a little sport, creative activity and, later, popular theology, the *basis* of human affairs in the home and family unit was taken for granted, its wide variation not appreciated let alone understood, and its cumulative affects on the behaviour of others, let alone the self, not considered.

But this ignorance, so prevalent within the 'big science' community, has been reflected in much of the recent debate about educational performance in which the professional practices of the schools have been widely assumed to be solely responsible for the various abilities (linguistic, mathematical, scientific, and so on) of pupils. Yet, leaving aside the findings of research, every probation officer, social worker and school counsellor knows through case experience that factors

5

within home and family provide, for the majority, the foundations for emotional, social and intellectual adjustment as life progresses.

In this chapter, the content and nature of the research evidence concerning the origins and determinants of educational achievement will be briefly examined, along with some of the derived implications for educational policy. This is a natural area of concern for an educationist and, as we will see, aspects of life quite outside the control of the formal educational system as such exert powerful influences upon the attainment of objectives within it. Hence, educational accountability is irrevocably entwined with wider processes of social evaluation, central to which is the character of day-by-day care, security and stimulation given to and received by individuals in the home and family setting.

## THE COMPLEXITY OF EDUCATIONAL PERFORMANCE

Through the work of biologists and, more recently, psychologists, we now know that many of the everyday human actions and activities which we take for granted, such as talking, reading, driving, relating to other people, and checking our bank statement, are in reality extremely complicated when analysed in detail. They each embody a range of skills which become coordinated and orchestrated for successful performance.

Taking the example of reading, the process may not be adequately described in simple terms, but learning to read is to learn a system of rules and methods for extracting information from text. Pre-reading skills include the perception and analysis of speech sounds, the early production and discrimination of writing and graphic symbols, generating the appropriate eye movements, the matching of graphic displays with sounds and the learning of letter names. In the early reading phase, the child must realise that word patterns carry meaning and must be individually decoded and checked against the sense of the sentence context, which is often a matter of trial and error. The noticing of the structures within words and the acquisition of a range of spelling patterns is also important at this stage. In the transition to skilled reading, phonic rules for spelling are learned, subvocalisation develops as an aid to comprehension, and eye movements and fixations become more adapted to the text in hand and its grammatical form so that more advanced and faster decoding skills are acquired. The later, more mature and economic development of reading abilities depends upon the growth of active and flexible word recognition and processing strategies which adapt to meet the demands of new text in the light of the reader's informational needs, such as obtaining the gist of the printed text or remembering detail.

Thus, if we give a child a standardised reading test we are measuring in reality a multitude of abilities, including their coordination and the child's social confidence to respond in the testing situation. Hence, if we ask questions regarding the particular influences which *caused* reading performance of a specific level, or promoted differences in reading achievement between children of the same age, it has to be appreciated that these are many and are likely to vary significantly between individuals.

Similar complexities of possible causal interactions are encountered in most other areas of school performance from mathematics achievement through the development of social, religious and moral attitudes, to skill in sports or crafts. For some outcomes, particularly in the realm of attitudes, there are in addition large problems in defining precisely and reliably the nature of the measured 'performances', let alone in relating them to possible determining factors.

It is crucial to recognise that upon the base of genetic 'natural' endowment is written a 'nurtural' history unique for each child (even for identical twins) which it is difficult, if not impossible, for the most generously funded educational research to monitor unambiguously and relate as causes to a range of measured performances using representative samples of children.

## NATURE AND NURTURE

The influence of genetic endowment (heredity) on the one hand, and the influence of the surroundings (environment) on the other, in the determination of educational achievement has been the subject of debate, and even bitter controversy, ever since genetics emerged as an essential strand in biological science in the early years of this century. Rapid progress has been made in this field, and the processes by which the hereditary material, the genes, derived equally from the male and female parents, determines and organises the development of the embryo from the fertilised egg through successive stages to its mature form are now quite well understood. There is good evidence, too, that mental and even emotional characteristics in man are determined in much the same way as the more easily studied physical traits in experimental plants and animals, not excluding man. The processes are essentially the same throughout the entire living world.

What is important to appreciate here is that these developmental processes require at each step the appropriate environment in which the genes that control them can operate. In the earliest stages these requirements are precise and specific, and development proceeds or fails according to whether they are met or not. Later, and especially at the higher levels of organisation, there is more room for variation. Increasingly development responds differentially to different conditions; the environment in which the genes do their work is no longer specific, it offers alternative degrees of action, until in man acting at the highest level of all, that of consciousness, the problem of individual free will within a framework of biological and social conditioning has to be faced. That cannot be a central concern here, but it does emphasise the fact, basic to the later discussion, that heredity and environment cannot act in isolation. They are interdependent. Expressed succinctly, heredity determines potentiality, the environment defines the extent to which these potentialities are realised in practice. As Sir J.A. Thompson used to express it in the early days of the heredity/environment debate: 'If Beethoven had been born into a tribe of Patagonian Indians he would not have composed his symphonies but he would have been the best tom-tom player in the tribe.'

It follows that when considering the determinants of educational achievement cognisance must be taken of both genetic endowment and the provision of suitable learning environments. What comprises the most suitable environment for any given individual (genotype) introduces the large measure of uncertainty which confronts alike the educationist and the social scientist.

In regard to some characteristics, genetics sets well-defined limits; in others, there is much more room for manoeuvre. This statement introduces the concept of heritability so important in animal breeding programmes and in respect of any trait that results from the cumulative effects of many genes. It is probably true to say that the area of intellectual development affords much more opportunity for variation under the influence of the environment than was at one time thought possible.

There has been a strong swing towards this viewpoint in recent years, and this has been linked to programmes of social reform disseminated through the educational services, intended to reduce gross differences in social opportunity between different sectors of the population, and especially between social classes and between native British and ethnic minorities. However, it is worth remembering that environmental factors are varied and their effects cumulative. Homes, schools and other influences can be mutually supportive, lacking in common direction, or frankly antagonistic. Their effects are not easily separable and the researcher, concerned with generalisation and long-term objectives, has to do the best he can with the always limited data he is able to collect about the lives of individuals.

## THE CONTEXT OF POLICY-RELEVANT RESEARCH

Much of the educational research to be summarised below leads to the conclusion that, compared with other influences, amongst which the family and the home rank very high, schools make a relatively small contribution to variations in educational achievement. How justified is this conclusion, which seems to undermine a good deal of popular faith in formal education and to deny the commonsense experience of individual teachers, parents and pupils?

At least part of the answer lies in the origin, purpose and scope of the research. In general, research is not concerned, as are parents and teachers, with individual children and short-term objectives, the attainment of which are subtle, ill-defined and not amenable to quantification and mass assessment. Much educational research sets out to identify broad principles and trends that will enable policy makers and administrators to make decisions leading to what they regard as desirable long-term ends. Researchers, therefore, are concerned with populations of children, not individual children, and so, at the genetic level, with gene pools (the total gene composition of the population) and not with individual genotypes (the genetic endowment of individuals).

Both gene pools and genotypes interact with their respective environments, but their study and experimental manipulation require different techniques which, when applied to man, raise moral and ethical issues which effectively prohibit experimentation. Educational research thus has to rely largely on cross-sectional or longitudinal survey techniques or, on rare occasions, on so-called 'natural experiments', in which some control of the operational conditions has been provided without deliberate interference.

LARGE SCALE SURVEYS

Over the past fifteen years, with the extension of the range of computer analyses possible with multivariate social science data, a number of large-scale surveys of educational performance have been executed with the intention of illuminating policies which might improve educational practice and increase the 'returns' to the community from what, in the context of any country or region, must always be a finite educational budget. Amongst these studies, two (one by Coleman and co-workers in the USA and the other in England for the Plowden Report) were large national surveys concerned with the concept of equality of educational opportunity as a means of effecting social change towards a more equal and just society. A third, which included studies in seven subject areas (mathematics, reading comprehension, literature, science, English and French as foreign languages, and civic education) was conducted under the aegis of the International Association for the Evaluation of Educational Achievement (IEA) and was concerned more with those factors which operate across various aspects of the curriculum and across national boundaries.

All these studies, perhaps not surprisingly, showed up the importance of home background, and what was rather unexpected, the comparative unimportance of the school, which was often outweighed tenfold or more by home background. The latter was found even in those subjects such as science, modern languages and civic education which appear on the surface to be much more school-dependent than others, such as mother-tongue fluency.

In the present context, the survey for the Plowden primary education Report is of special significance, since the collection of data for statistical analysis was only part of a very much wider study involving interviews with parents as well as the usual tests and questionnaires. The data were collected at three primary school age-levels and the outcome variable 'on trial' was the result of a reading comprehension test with, in the case of the top infants, a picture intelligence test. Of the variation of scores *between* schools which could be accounted for, 'parental attitudes' (28%) was most important, followed by variables associated with 'home circumstances' (20%), and then those associated with the 'state of the school' (17%). These figures leave no doubt about the importance of home background in the early stages of schooling, and since relatively fixed variables like parents' occupation, material circumstances and level of education seemed to account for only about a quarter of the parental attitudes component, it was argued that the latter could be altered by persuasive educational initiatives with parents. A significant decline in each of the 'parental attitudes' (20%) and 'home circumstances' (9%) contributions to score variations in the *within* schools analysis demonstrated a clear neighbourhood uniformity effect. This helped to lead to the 'educational priority area' (EPA) policies deisgned to help compensate for home and community educational deficits and thus promote a greater equality of opportunity.

A number of critical reappraisals of the large scale survey studies have more recently taken place using improved statistical techniques. For example, Jencks' reassessment of the 1960s research has the following carefully worded phrase which incorporates both genetic and environmental components:

> . . . variations in what children learn in school depend largely on variations in what they bring to school, not in variations in what schools offer them.

The emphasis on variations is also intentional; if there is little variation between schools, then their influence is bound to be less statistically than that of other factors in which there is greater variation. Jencks goes on to write:

> There seems, for example, to be an association between the amount a mother talks to her child and the child's subsequent verbal skills. If talking to the child is interesting and pleasant, most mothers will talk more than if the child is inarticulate. If the child's verbal responses to its mother are affected by its genes, as seems likely, then the mother's dealings with the child will also end up being determined partly by the child's genes.

This is a good example of the indirect action of genes through an apparently environmental factor. A small genetic advantage may thus progressively produce subsequent environmental advantages, and of course vice versa. Effects of this kind appear in heritability calculations as so-called 'interaction effects'.

As a result of this very thorough study not only of the Coleman data, but also those of many other studies, including the Plowden Report, the authors assign, *as a general indication only,* the following values to the three general contributions to educational achievement based on the amount of variance they are able to 'explain' in multivariate regression analysis studies.

*Genetic* (under random environmental conditions) 45% (33% to 50%)

*Environmental* (under random genetical conditions) 35% (25% to 40%)

*Interaction effects* about 20%

Conventional wisdom suggests that the order is about right, and that in ensuring that every child has the opportunity to make the most of his innate abilities, whether intellectually or in other directions, the importance of the family and the home are unquestionable, and are certainly not merely marginal in their influence. Let us look at an example.

Some relatively recent reanalysis at Aston of our IEA science achievement data for fourteen-year-olds indicates a complex network of relationships in which the cluster of significant home background variables (fathers' occupation, mothers' level of education, and, negatively, family size) are shown to be important for the eighteen countries in this almost entirely school-focused subject. Figure 1 is a path diagram which shows in outline the major relationships between the significant variables: the range of values possible for the figures is –100 to +100 and a minus sign denotes a negative relationship.

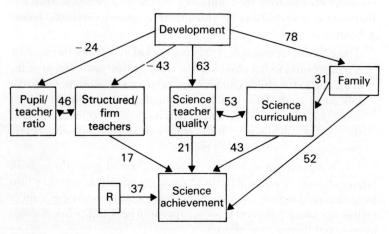

1   *Path diagram showing presumed causal relationships (straight lines) between variables promoting science achievement at fourteen plus in eighteen countries; curved lines denote non-causal significant correlations. (86% of variance explained; R = residual or other unidentified factors.)*

The blocks within Figure 1 are defined as follows in an approximate through-time sequence:

*Development*     an index of each country's economic development
= gross national product per capita + % of workforce
employed in non-agricultural occupations ÷ 2

*Family*     an index of the family as an educational resource = % of
fathers in professional/managerial occupations + years of
mothers' education – number of children in the family ÷ 3

*School variables*     four blocks as shown, with science teacher quality and science curriculum being composites of eight separate
variables (four each)

The interpretation of Figure 1 is briefly thus. National economic
development sets limits to both the development of formal educational
systems and the family as an educational resource. Hence strong
relationships are shown between development and family, lower
pupil/teacher ratios, teacher quality and the availability of a good
range of science curriculum activities for pupils. Interestingly, it
appears that economic development results in a tendency towards less
structured teacher/pupil relationships as a whole, yet these are not so
conducive as are more rule-bound or authoritative classroom regimes
for the range of science achievements measured by our IEA tests. Only
the pupil/teacher ratio variable fails to have a significant *direct* causal
link with achievement, a finding in line with many other large-scale
studies, and one which is too complex an issue to discuss here. Given,
however, a straight choice between using a fixed amount of resources
for either reducing pupil/teacher ratios in schools or improving the
family situation as an educational and development resource, there is
much evidence which would prompt the latter.

Pupils' 'liking of school' is also, and not surprisingly, a significant
factor in promoting school achievement, and when this variable is
inserted in the IEA science data analysis, a more complex picture
emerges, the core of which is shown in Figure 2 (found on page 14).
Here the most striking relationships between 'development' and
'family' with 'liking school' act in a counterbalanced way which
reduces the size of the direct causal paths to 'science achievement'.

Results of the IEA work and a number of other strands of research in
science education suggest in summary that if science achievement is to
be maximised in a country, political and educational policy needs to
be directed towards:

increasing economic development, encouraging smaller families,

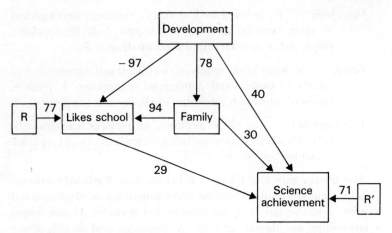

2  *Simplified path diagram for science achievement incorporating the 'likes school' variable but excluding the four school blocks of Figure 1. (50% of variance explained; R, R' = residual factors.)*

improving the educational sensitivity and attitudinal support of the home by attention especially to mothers' education, raising the quality of the science teaching force, increasing the curricular time devoted to science and the range of science experience facilities available, while, without making school an unpleasant, inhuman and overbearing environment, encouraging teachers to be reasonably demanding, structured and authoritative in their professional style.

This discussion, in which science achievement has merely been taken as an example area, indicates that while, for various technical reasons associated with the statistical analyses of large scale surveys, the effects of school-based variables may not have been sufficiently emphasised in some studies, being swamped by the greater variability in circumstances external to the school, policies inherent in schools are important. A recent study by Wagenaar of the effects of structural and contextual variables upon achievement in 135 elementary schools in the USA found conclusively that 'school permeability', that is the level of interaction between schools and their environments, is positively related to school achievement independently of the socioeconomic status of the school and many aspects of its internal organisation. In other words, involvement of school with parents and community and vice versa, thereby promoting a greater cohesiveness of their intentions, attitudes and objectives, is beneficial to children's performance.

The school's permeability to its surrounding adult community enshrines quite naturally potential aspects of parent education which will be referred to in Chapter 5.

SCHOOL CASE STUDIES

No one style of educational research can provide all the necessary insights for policy making. More intensive analysis of school processes, in addition to the perhaps often somewhat crude measures of input and output used in large scale surveys, is possible through the use of the case study approach. Schools serving apparently similar neighbourhoods and having broadly similar capital and recurrent resources for a given age range can develop very differently in terms of internal organisation and visible 'ethos', not least as a result of the influence over time of the teaching staff, and in particular, the headteacher. It is now clear that individual differences between schools in terms of emphasis and process can produce quite marked differences in outcome measures such as academic achievement, the realisation of career prospects, juvenile delinquency and school attendance.

Rutter's recently reported five year longitudinal study of a dozen London comprehensive schools involving 3500 pupils who comprised the 1971 intake vividly illustrates that while schools may not be the most powerful shaping environment for ranges of educational performance in our society, they are nonetheless vitally important. In Rutter's excellently designed study, the criterion measures were not limited to educational achievement, but included behaviour in school, attendance, and behaviour out of school. It thus took into account some of the objectives that schools set for themselves besides educational achievement. The Inner London Education Authority (ILEA) grades pupils on secondary school entry into three bands of ability, Band 1 or high (top 25%); Band 2 or medium (middle 50%); and Band 3 or low (bottom 25%), on the basis of verbal reasoning scores at age 10. In Figure 3 (page 16) the schools are ranked according to the success achieved by the middle band in the external examinations taken five years later.

Figure 3 shows amongst other things that the best school achieved as good results with pupils initially determined as being of low ability as the worst school achieved with pupils of high ability, and that the pattern of results for each school is broadly similar in all three bands.

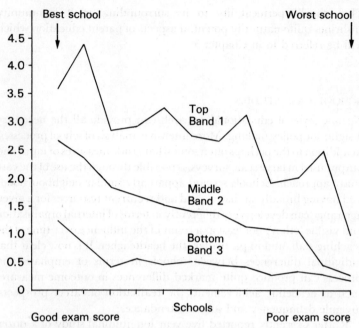

3  *Weighted average examination scores in twelve secondary schools*

Furthermore, differences between the schools, which were generally working under unpromising social conditions, could not be explained by intake variations in verbal reasoning and parental occupation, and broadly similar results were obtained when behaviour and attendance were studied. Schools do indeed matter, and success breeds success.

What perhaps mattered most for this context, however, is that praise and encouragement achieved better results than over-strict discipline, when judged both by examination results and by behaviour. Providing a pleasant and stimulating environment also helped, as did giving pupils a measure of personal responsibility. These are matters in which home and school can obviously cooperate so that, rather than seeking to apportion credit (or blame) to influences outside school, regarded as quite beyond association with what goes on inside school, *efforts to increase the interaction between them would seem to be a wiser policy.* There can be no doubt that good home influence makes a vital contribution to children's all-round development as well as to their educational achievement. It could be greater still if made jointly in more explicit cooperation with their schools, as intended by the visionaries of community education, such as Henry Morris in the 1930s in Cambridgeshire.

## FAMILY FUNCTIONING WITH SCHOOL?

This brief description of research has pointed to the significant and interdependent roles of home and school in promoting educational performance. It also prompts the drawing of possible parallels between the two environments. The good school may be described as a well-organised environment which expects good standards, where the teachers provide good models of behaviour, and where the pupils are praised and given responsibility; it is not a harassed, unpredictable and inconsistent institution in which expectations are uncertain. And a lot of professional training and experience goes into the building and maintenance of a good school. The effective home situation likewise is one which provides predictable and consistent loving care for all the family members, in which parents set good examples of behaviour, and in which there is a warm and respectful security. In much the same way as teachers need to be helped to do their jobs effectively, so we may wonder if, in today's complex society, sufficient effective homes can be created simply through instinct. No less than schools, homes are buffeted by many forces not under their direct control.

Thus any concerted long-term attack on the problems of educational inequality must include attention to policies relating to what happens inside families and not simply to facets of formal education. The enormous residual faith in the school as an instrument of social change must be tempered by the recognition of the family and the community as at least equal contributors. We now know that schools *alone* can never be significant agents in reducing social injustice and inequality, for they cannot repair all the problems derivative from difficult home and neighbourhood circumstances. While a good school can modify the behaviour and improve the attainment of all its pupils, it cannot even up the unequal educational chances of pupils from different family backgrounds. Educational opportunities offered to children require a corresponding reciprocity in home and neighbourhood if they are to be completely effective, for schools are, for the majority of their pupils, agents of affirmation of many traits derivative from the parental lottery at the 'accident' of birth. We must be concerned with making good schools even better, but good homes also need fostering through a range of policies, some of which must utilise and adapt existing educational resources. There is certainly sufficient environmental influence upon educational performance to encourage us in more coherent social endeavours for the sake of children.

We have seen that family background is an important ingredient in the determination of a child's educational achievement. Educational achievement, broadly interpreted, can in its turn be a potent factor in the stability and harmony of family life; alternatively, failure can be a disturbing and disruptive influence. The interdependence of home, school and community must eventually be translated into a blurring of their formal boundaries, particularly at the non-specialist stages up to the age of sixteen. Furthermore, the problems and skills of parenthood and running a home must be understood as much as those of teaching and school administration if more effective cooperation between home and school is to be achieved, upon a basis of mutual respect and shared values. We now turn in the next chapter to the nature of the parental task within the framework of family life.

## References

BRIMER, A, *et al.* (1978). *Sources of Difference in School Achievement.* Slough: NFER Publishing.

COLEMAN, J. S., *et al.* (1966). *Equality of Educational Opportunity.* Washington, D.C.: U.S. Government Printing Office.

COMBER, L. C., and KEEVES, J. P. (1973). *Science Education in Nineteen Countries.* IEA: Stockholm: Almqvist and Wiksell, and New York and Chichester: John Wiley.

GIBSON, E. J., and LEVIN, H. (1975). *The Psychology of Reading.* Cambridge, Mass.: MIT Press.

JENCKS, C., *et al.* (1972). *Inequality—a reassessment of the effect of family and schooling in America.* Harmondsworth: Penguin Books.

MILLER, G. W. (1971). *Educational Opportunity and the Home.* Harlow: Longman.

RUTTER, M., *et al.* (1979). *Fifteen Thousand Hours.* London: Open Books.

WAGENAAR, T. C. (1978). In *Sociology and Social Research,* 62 (4), pp. 608–25.

WALKER, D. A. (1977). *Six Subject Survey: Study of Educational Achievement in 21 Countries.* IEA: Stockholm: Almqvist and Wiksell, and New York and Chichester: John Wiley.

WHITFIELD, R. C. (1976). 'Curriculum Planning, Teaching and Educational Accountability.' *Aston Educational Enquiry Monograph No. 6.* Birmingham: University of Aston.

WHITFIELD, R. C. (1979). 'Educational Research and Science Teaching' in *School Science Review,* 60 (212), pp. 411–30.

| # The Family Context for the Parental Task

*'Before I got married I had six theories about bringing up children; now I have six children and no theories.'*

The Second Earl of Rochester (1647–80)

*'As the sapling has been bent so will it grow.'*

The Seventh Earl of Shaftesbury (1801–85)

'Wait until you have children: your life will never be the same' is a true statement if ever there was one, even though many cases of child neglect reflect parental attempts to sustain earlier lifestyles. The coming of children produces great changes—in family economics, in sleeping and eating patterns, in property ownership, in leisure and holidays. Suddenly too the new parent is thrust into the role of being the child's first teacher, not simply for later skills like tieing shoelaces, kicking a ball or riding a bicycle, but for much more subtle things, often at the outer margins of awareness, in the development of language, of social attitudes and moral behaviour.

The parental task is helping this child to become a person, and the lesson lasts throughout the totality of care—now no less than about a twenty-year task. No bells of respite are rung as at the end of the 40-minute school period, and a willingness to work nightshifts is essential! Yet parental teaching requires energy and time. To forget to teach, to be too tired to teach, or to opt out of teaching does not remove the task; it simply changes the lesson, for apathy and indifference are both caught and taught.

Generally speaking, before a system of universal state education system is introduced the nuclear family or the 'tribe' (extended family) have made themselves responsible for handing on the essential skills for living and survival, so that the notion of the 'family school' is not new. Despite the formalisation of much of the educational process, work habits, learning styles, values, and relationships with authority figures continue to be learned first and most naturally in the family setting.

Raising a family has been strikingly and correctly likened to the setting up of a short production run of a high quality article in which prototypes are excluded and mistakes are costly and may be largely irreversible. To pursue the analogy further, it is nevertheless suggested later that 'firms' can reduce their risks through acquiring information and understanding about the principles of the 'production process'; we shall be doing this within the context of a map of Education for Parenthood.

## DEFINITION AND DIVERSITY OF FAMILY LIFE

In this text it is not appropriate to define the family narrowly, nor in the phrases used by sociologists, for our concern is essentially with the care of children and, concomitantly with the well-being of the adults who care for them. Hence a family is here viewed simply as a relatively small group of people in which one or more dependent children are being cared for by one or more adults within some kind of defined home territory. This stresses the role of the family as a cohabiting unit of social organisation for the day by day caring and rearing of children, and excludes other social groupings which can in some real sense claim to be families, such as the childless family group, or the extended three-generation family, or even a church congregation.

This definition is however inclusive of a range of structures and of styles, since in our society we need to consider not only the standard two-parent family but also the fostering or adoptive family, the single-parent family, the second-marriage family and even the experimental commune. Within these there are of course the rich and the poor, the happy and the troubled, the only-child to the many-child family. Each of these has developed a variety of styles of living, and although at least on the surface the Judao-Christian tradition of family life remains significant in the majority of western households with men still being the more dominant, other religious and ethnic traditions must now be respected in our developing multiracial and multicultural society. However, even before the arrival of the Commonwealth immigrant communities, Britain had a rich diversity of styles of family life derivative from different attitudes towards and practice of roles within the family according to sex, geographical location, occupation, housing and economic status. It is crucial to recognise that our concern with the effective care of children within families does not imply a uniformity of pattern or approach; indeed our distinctiveness and dignity as individuals derives in part from the subtleties and diversities of our life-styles.

Within the inevitable and welcome diversities, however, we must, insofar as children are concerned, emphasise some predominant values, that is the foundation ethics of parenthood and child care. Firstly there should be a basic respect, built upon awareness, for the rights, needs and individuality of each child, in particular the child's right to continuous and dependable loving care. Secondly, there should be a genuine and pervasive commitment to the responsibilities of child-rearing, at least to the point at which the child has grown to a stage of relative autonomy and has acquired a sufficient measure of social and economic independence. The child's rights and the caregiver's obligations and responsibilities go hand in hand and are parts of the same piece.

This ethical framework is not however prescriptive regarding the detail of parental or other long-term caregiver action, in the sense that there is no 'right' way to bring up children. However, our increased understanding of children through the work of sociologists, psychologists, anthropologists, educationists and the medical profession suggests that there are some basic needs to be met in a child's everyday life whatever the particular context of the family. The rights of children can today be more sensitively expressed than in the past, and the responsibilities of parents have therefore become more sophisticated. This may be illustrated by two examples.

Poliomyelitis can cripple children: we now have a very safe preventive measure for it, and provided parents know about this (and here is an imperative for the educational services) they have a responsibility to ensure that their children are vaccinated. We know that children's language and motor development can be severely limited if they are not spoken to or provided with opportunities for play on a regular basis during the first three years of life: hence responsible parenthood will create frequent opportunities for such activities, whatever the lifestyle. The first example prescribes a specific act of parental care, while the second dictates a general principle which leaves open a wide variety of acts for its implementation. The history of fads and fashions among child care experts has often arisen from their succumbing to the temptation to be too specific about ways in which parents should act. Controversies among experts, for example on breast versus bottle feeding, on potty training and corporal punishment, still reflect their individual wish to generalise behaviour beyond the limits of both their breadth of experience and the evidence available. Sometimes differences in experts' views derive from shrouded divergencies in objectives and ethics regarding the minutiae of child care rather than an evaluation of scientific evidence. Children, parents and their family circumstances are so varied as to make unjustified the advocacy of specific orthodoxies of child care.

Despite its potential for variation in child-rearing, the family has not been short of its critics in recent years. Some psychiatrists have emphasised the destructive and repressive potential of the family, suggesting that it can distort life and lead to suffering and neurotic conflict through the abuse of its implicit power structures. The women's movement has seen the family as essentially exploitive of the female identity, while other factions have viewed stable marriages and families as basically a conservative means of perpetuating the *status quo*, the class structure, inequalities and blind obedience to capitalist-style authority. The family is thus held responsible for inhibiting movements towards a more just, open, less divisive and less prejudiced society. Edmund Leach in his 1967 Reith Lectures made the following stark and unscholarly comment which sums up some of these views:

> The family looks inward upon itself; there is an intensification of emotional stress between husband and wife, and parents and children. The strain is more than most of us can bear. Far from being the basis of the good society, the family, with its privacy and tawdry secrets, is the source of all our discontents.

There is naturally some truth even in such global criticisms. The family may be too enclosed, even in a Christian context, for both children and parents. Many children have found their home lives excessively constricting and have had their identities deformed through the insensitivities of their generally unaware parents. Many parents experience a loss of freedom, and find their home lives constrained in terms of the wider legitimate development of adult relationships; a possessive exclusiveness tends to stand in the way of the satisfaction of the wider needs for companionship. Can so-called 'affairs', presently experienced, according to a recent estimate (Lake and Hills 1979), by over half of all married couples, simply be categorised as unwarranted deviance? Or do they reflect, at least in part, the unfulfilled needs of individuals for whom accepting love has seemed a scarce commodity? However, the critics of the family rarely propose or suggest practicable alternatives, and the dilemma always remains regarding the central question: who else in a democratic society will care on a long-term basis for the majority of children other than their parents? The early transfer of children to communal creches in the USSR has been abandoned, and parallel developments expanding the role of parents in Israeli *Kibbutzim* are also taking place.

The familial is the familiar, that which defines, orders and maintains the personal world, and the familiar is essential to all of us, and especially to children growing up. If family life from time to time breeds a degree of suffocation, it nevertheless can provide a steady ritual of the everyday in which some of the most profound satisfactions and confidences can lie. The family may thus potentially be truly a 'haven in a heartless world', providing, amid seas of uncertainty, the boundaries of order and a measure of predictability without which life would not be bearable. The family can both sustain, stabilise and liberate all its members—given the chance by both government and community together with a generally deeper knowledge of interpersonal needs.

But in living in an active community such as a family, there must inevitably be some constraints upon the operation of personal choice. This rubs hard against the modern doctrines of near-mandatory self-actualisation, distorted to the point at which the total social context tends to be disregarded. Corporate living involves in part the abandonment of some purely personal goals, ambitions and satisfactions, and must take on board the paradox that the greatest personal growth may often result from considering others rather than being anxious about one's own welfare and personality development. The quest for self-actualisation can become akin to a kind of psychological hypochondria, and, if practised intensively within the context of family life, can become an alarming form of selfishness. It is by no means far fetched to suggest that some of those keen on the demise of the family are simply trying to escape from a context in which the inevitable frailities of human nature are laid bare; for human nature is muddled, and its inconsistencies—such as strength and weakness, love and hate, tenderness and temper—are so visible at close quarters in a family setting. In many other spheres of life we are able to cover up our weaknesses and avoid letting others know of our true selves. This is not so easily done within the family, for in living with each other we can come to know each other. But by knowing and having many of our privacies invaded, while being provided with sufficient freedom to establish our identity, we may respond more lovingly and sensitively than is ever possible within many fundamentally less durable social structures.

Fundamentally this is not to take a romanticised view of family life, but a realistic one. Certainly to take a stance which implies that we have ever had, and have now lost, a 'golden age' of the family (a dream shared by both Left and Right) is to ignore many of the more recent findings of British social historians, such as Laslett's Cambridge-based group. What seems clear is that individual psychological security in our kind of society is likely to depend for the forseeable future upon forms of social organisation which develop intimacy and confidence, and aim to provide the long-term care of people for each other in relatively small, stable groups.

## COMMITMENT BETWEEN PARENTS

The discharging of the tasks of parenthood and the stability and consistency of the care provided for children is made easier or more difficult according to the nature of the relationship between the parents. While parental relationships, like all others, are rarely static, the level of confidence and dependability that each partner holds for the other conditions the climate for child rearing. Insecure parents confused about their long-term goals and commitments are likely to create insecure home environments for their offspring. With the demise of arranged relationships, dowries and settlements, individuals now have considerable autonomy in the choice of their partner for cohabitation or for marriage. Hence, at least some of the foundations for effective child care may be worked out, or ignored, during courtship.

Despite the ease with which divorce has now become available, marriage as an acceptable state for men and women remains attractive. A congenial marriage can provide more contentment and emotional security than any other relationship, and the ancient trinity of father, mother and child, depicted by artists down the ages, has survived more vicissitudes than other human relationships. It has been vividly commented that in any future *Götterdammerung* which nuclear abuse and lack of statesmanship may be preparing for us, the last man will spend his last hours searching for his wife and child. For both sexes, at least the possibility of marriage remains on the agenda, even though many probably fear that they, apparently like increasing numbers of their neighbours, may not be successful at building a permanently rewarding one. Yet success is more likely to grow out of confident commitment than hesitancy.

Heterosexual friendships often quickly ripen into courtship, so that the conditions which facilitate such friendships may also lead to partnership. Hence marriages tend to be within the same social groups and institutions within those groups, such as attendances at the same church or sports club, or involvement in some shared interest or activity. An element of chance enters in and the stages are progressive. Conscious efforts may or may not be made by the couple themselves to assess their suitability; they are frequently made by one or both sets of their parents. This may lead to intergenerational conflict, for there is regrettably no widespread social commitment to marriage preparation, and couples can easily view unsolicited advice at this stage as insensitive interference. The belief that opposites attract one another or that complementary needs are satisfied has gained little investigational support. There seems to be a spontaneous attraction between the prospective partners, a product of inner drives, rather than deliberate choice or adjustment. Chance thus plays a decisive part in the rewards or frustrations, the success or failure of the marriage bond. Factors deemed by social scientists relevant to mate selection are, for example, contrasts between dominance and submissiveness, and between what is called nurturance and receptiveness (giving and receiving of sympathy), but probably more significant than the traits overtly assessed by psychologists is how couples *perceive* each other.

Courtship patterns have changed during the last few decades; there are fewer class differences, and in general men and women have different attitudes to sexual experiences, whether total or merely exploratory. Societal attitudes to pre-marital sexual experience also vary. In general, males are still allowed more freedom socially than females. Men of all social classes may tend to treat the sex act fairly lightly, as an end in itself; women associate it with the giving and receiving of love. American writers have simplisticly described men as body-centred, women as person-centred. Mutual respect and understanding of the totality of another person is the key to relationships, but this is often lacking, and the sexual revolution may strangely enough have favoured men rather than women, and women could now be more, rather than less, in danger of exploitation.

Nevertheless, the foundations of caring parenthood begin during courtship, and if this phase is approached with maturity, each couple will try to openly anticipate one another's frailties, aspirations, preferences and values, including attitudes towards childrearing. For most people at this stage educational help is necessary, not only to help structure discussion and understanding, but to assist couples in being realistic at a time of exciting romantic exploration. The ideal agenda during this period is impossible to prescribe, but should include all major topics over which later tensions and alienation could arise, such as money and material possessions, sex, work and holidays, leisure activities, religious and political beliefs, in addition perhaps to more specific aspects of homemaking and child care. Just as later on avenues of communication between parents and children become important, between the courting couple they are vital to the whole future of their family. One of the difficulties which many parents experience subsequent to the arrival of children is the invasion of the privacy of their relationship. This can make it hard for parents to remain in close communication, and can thus place the foundation relationship of the family, often unknowingly, at risk through a subtle drifting apart.

In our kind of society unmarried parentage can be psychologically disturbing to both child and parent. Hence, it is desirable for children to be blessed by legal marital status between their parents, if only to avoid any stigma of being different among their peers; despite more widespread social tolerance, being born out of wedlock remains for some a disadvantage. Equally, if not more important, is the intention of the parents to endeavour to make their union strong and permanent, based upon love, respect, toleration and mutual fulfilment rather than simply duty. However, with the arrival of children the increased responsibilities quite naturally lay upon parents an increased sense of duty which should not necessarily be disparaged; the presence of children has seen some couples through times of crisis to the eventual benefit of the whole family. Of course divorce exists as an essential safety valve for those who turn out to be incompatible or who regrettably drift apart, and in cases where the married relationship has resulted in considerable turmoil which is also experienced continuously by the children, divorce can be a real blessing for all concerned. Nonetheless, the intention of giving permanence to the male/female relationship still seems the only responsible basis for the birth of children, and a framework of promises or covenants remains a necessary part of such an intention. Yet the difficulties of keeping such promises in a society which lacks a consensus about relationships and is inherently volatile must not be minimised. Within our social confusion the possibility of some insincerity (or lack of self-knowledge while promising) can be real. To promise sincerely is of course to take a risk, but one which is responsible if based upon mutual knowledge and understanding; defective promising is irresponsible and damaging.

## CHANGES OF LIFESTYLE AND ROLE DELINEATION

Marriage traditionally meant a turning point in lifestyle. Nowadays with the woman and the man often working and living away from their parental homes, perhaps even living together beforehand, and then both working after marriage to establish themselves economically, sometimes without ever a honeymoon to mark the change in status, the onset of parenthood has become the real turning point. This is followed by new constraints, new loyalties and new duties, which education for parenthood (see Chapter 5) could help both to anticipate and to initiate the adaptive capabilities of the new parents.

We know relatively little about how couples cope with the transition to parenthood in contemporary society, nor about the ranges of support which would be most useful to them. What is clear, however, is that this period is crucial to the long-term well-being of both couple and child. The mother's physical and emotional health is particularly vital, as are her wider relationships which help to foster the early bonding and acceptance of the new child within the whole family. The roles and actions of the father during the transition to parenthood are largely uncharted, but his potential for various kinds of supporting role is significant at a time at which the infant is a lusty competitor for attention from his spouse. For both father and mother the extra role as parent, with new responsibilities within the tasks of homemaking, is indeed significant, superimposed as it is upon other likely continuing parallel roles as citizen, worker, spouse and individual. Anticipation of these new demands can never be complete, but many still stumble into parenthood, only rapidly to discover some of its stark and possibly unwanted realities. Here, for example, is a young mother talking about her acquired role:

'I never thought about it before . . . you know about being a mother . . . being married. I thought you'd have more freedom when you're married because you've only got your husband to tell you what to do and you can stand up to him. . . But with the children, I never really thought about it till he came. . . Well I just thought it would be like when I was single and we'd go on holiday together and get home at night just when we wanted. I never really thought about having children—and having to look after them— and stop going to work. It never occurred to me . . . I used to plan and look forward to things, like going out and getting dressed up, but now I've got the children things hit me at the last minute . . . it's just one mad rush. I don't seem to think about anything really much, and my husband says I've changed because I don't think about things outside the house. All I can think about is babies, babies and children and sort of how to keep nappies clean and sort of boring things like that.'

Within this mother's graphic description one senses feelings of captivity, of low self-esteem, and perhaps of resentment that nobody made her think through some of the fundamental realities before she and her husband took on responsibilities which they now must shoulder, apparently somewhat alone.

The detail of roles enacted by the new parents is likely to vary significantly according to domestic circumstances, particularly family income, housing, the developmental difficulties of the child (such as sleep habits and illness), and the network of support 'external' to the home unit which is available, whether through friends and relatives, or statutory agencies and voluntary groups. When state maternity benefits cease to be payable, the need for augmented family income is likely to be the first consideration underlying decisions regarding one or both parents' participation in the employment market, with considerations such as personal satisfaction and fulfilment usually taking second place. In addition, there are implicit and explicit expectations upon mother and father arising from their respective cultural backgrounds. Although we have entered a phase of questioning many aspects of sex roles, expectations remain for most significantly dependent upon geographical location, age, social class origin, level of education and occupation; and those expectations form a conditioning backcloth for the practice and decisions of the individual couple.

Probably the most significant factor in changing family lifestyles is the broadening of the feminine role. Many women now freed from much household drudgery by the products of domestic technology, and from the fear of incessant pregnancies by birth control techniques, are playing an increasing role in the family economy, aided by growing male cooperation in routine household tasks. Nevertheless, the male's need for job success is still deeply rooted in our society, and the biological obligations and 'inconveniences' for women remain if our species is to be maintained. The feminist movement, in arguing for the elimination of discriminating cultural differences superimposed upon and growing from the biological ones, has implicitly devalued the role of mothers in child-rearing and magnified their undoubted potential as members of the workforce external to the home.

Several surveys have indicated significant dissatisfaction among mothers of young children who stay at home full-time as housewives. Such negative feelings can hardly be satisfactory for the children, and suggest a need for support. This could either help mothers to perceive more clearly the importance and rewards of caring for their children, thereby compensating for the inevitable frustrations associated with childrearing, or by the sharing of care with others. If the latter is adopted there are obvious advantages in the father taking an appropriate share of child care by mutual agreement if compatible employment arrangements can be made. The structure of employment and careers presently closes the latter option except in rare cases; families and children are forced to adapt to the needs of employment rather than the reverse. Hence the demand for childminders, day nurseries and nursery education far outstrips the personnel and places presently available, and a combination of real or perceived economic need and task dissatisfaction leaves inevitable gaps in child care and facilities. The extent of this problem is further alluded to in the next chapter, but here we may note that nationally sampled survey data for 1976 indicated that over twice as many mothers with preschool age children would go out to work and share the tasks of childrearing with outsiders if they felt that adequate alternative care was available. Of the 900,000 mothers of the under-fives (out of a total of 3.4 million) who in 1976 were in paid employment, local authority day nurseries accommodated 30,000 of their children, while a further 30,000 were catered for in private nurseries and 90,000 were placed with registered childminders. This leaves a large gap in provision which is only partly filled by fathers, relatives, friends and neighbours, and it is at least a debatable point as to whether the State should step in with more parental substitute provision or give supportive help to parents themselves to enable them to operate in that role more satisfactorily and resolutely.

The role of fathers in the care of their children is likely to gain increased attention in future. There is some evidence to suggest that some fathers are effectively more distanced from child care than they might wish to be, sometimes finding it difficult to convey their real affection to their children and being excluded from much domestic decision-making. Yet in those families in which roles are truly shared by mother and father there are no indications that fathers cannot be just as nurturant as mothers, even with infants; only breast feeding is excluded in terms of innate ability to provide responsive care. It therefore seems that at least some of our assumptions regarding the primacy of the mother-infant relationship and the division of roles between the sexes have been more a product of cultural traditions than of innate endowments; and of course anthropological studies, such as those of Margaret Mead in Samoa and New Guinea, have charted successful child-rearing patterns quite distinct from the Western forms. But few in any group throw off the shackles of tradition overnight, since in any case these are a part of the individual and collective identity. Hence we might predict a continued gradual evolution of the fathering role from the earlier picture of the aloof Victorian male to one more of active nurturance by fathers of their young children, and to a greater sharing of both domestic responsibilities and breadwinning, preferably without depletion of the amount of time and energy which parents and children can spend and share together.

The increasing participation of fathers in the process of birth itself, despite the reticence of some medical staffs, is one example of change, and there is evidence for significant father preoccupation, absorption and interest in their newborn within the first three days of birth. Although it appears that infants can discriminate between fathers, mothers and strangers by about the age of three months, both laboratory and home-based studies suggest that infants of up to about one year do not have a consistent preference for either parent. Fathers are therefore important in their infants' cognitive and social development, including sex-typing, from a very early age. At present, however, in the pre-school years fathers spend only around one quarter of the time with their offspring that is spent with young children by their mothers, tending to participate mainly in play activities, leaving mothers to the more mundane aspects of child care. But fathers *can* care if they wish to, and *do* care if they have to.

As far as making decisions about shared care outside the nuclear family is concerned, parents need to appreciate that children, at least before puberty, derive security from attachment to a limited number of adult figures. It is important for them to find their environment predictable to enable new and confident learning, both social and 'academic', to take place at an optimum rate. Expert opinion varies regarding the number of adults with whom young children can feel secure, and this itself will vary according to the stage of development reached. Up to about the age of two to three secure attachment to one or two adults seems likely to be crucial in many cases if the infant is not to grow up into a person restricted in the ability to give affection. Time is needed for the development of all relationships at any stage. This is a necessary if not a sufficient condition for child care, and the more adults involved in it, the less time available for each to form secure reciprocal bonds with the child. Both child and adult need to feel some predictability and control over each other's behaviour. Without such a feeling children become cautious, even suspicious and distressed, and bearing in mind that children form relationships with adults before they do with their peers, early experiences of relationships with adults play a crucial part in their later adaptation in social situations. Certainly excessive multiple childminding, say beyond about four or five adults during any period of dependency, causes damage, as many cases of children 'in care' who have been frequently moved have shown. Hence working couples need to have satisfactory and stable alternative childminding arrangements in which the child both trusts and can sense their approval.

At this juncture in our social and economic development it seems generally unlikely that both parents will be able to have part-time careers in employment, thus giving to both fathers and mothers a wider variety of possible fulfilments, and to their children secure and refreshing attention from those most responsible for them. For parenting is fundamentally doing things *with* children rather than doing things *to* them or *for* them. The ever-precious commodity of undistracted *time* for interaction, for sharing, for conversation, and for measured stimulation in play, with books and on outings, remains crucial to its effectiveness. It may well be that the successful discharging of the parental role as it is now emerging cannot be expected to be carried out by one or two parents in relative isolation over the twenty-year period of committed care. Nonetheless, however the parental role is shared at various stages of child development—with teachers and other professionals, friends and relations—the bulk of responsibility will remain with the primary caregivers, that is most usually the natural parents. No child should be able to utter the bewildered lament:

Oh! Why does the wind blow upon me so wild?
Is it because I'm nobody's child?

STAGES IN CHILD CARE AND THE PARENTAL RESPONSE

We have indicated that children's lives and opportunities are not simply a product of their innate abilities and biological maturation, but are affected by both the expectations of the adults who are close to them and the mental, physical and emotional climates in which they are reared. Research in education and psychology has mapped in outline general stages of emotional and intellectual growth, and this largely substantiates the intuitive insights into child development which is evidenced in the history of children's literature. Much recent practice and innovation within education and social work reflects a helping, 'child-centred' philosophy because we now both comprehend and are endeavouring to provide for the needs of children as a whole, and that is a relatively new feature of Western culture.

Lloyd de Mause has charted six modes of parent-child relations in a continuous, overlapping and increasingly compressed historical sequence as parents slowly overcame their anxieties and developed the capacity to identify and meet the needs of their children. These modes range from infanticide in antiquity, through abandonment from about the fourth to the thirteenth centuries, than a period of 'ambivalence' before parents became in the eighteenth century 'intrusive' in style. The remaining 'socialising' and 'helping' modes do not emerge until the nineteenth and mid-twentieth centuries: the former (which is still popular and the source of psychological models such as behaviourism) is based upon a somewhat functional view of social relations and organisation, while the latter (so far consistently attempted only by a few) requires, in the words of de Mause:

... an enormous amount of time, energy, and discussion on the part of both parents ... for helping a young child reach its daily goals means continually responding to it, playing with it, tolerating its regressions, being its servant rather than the other way round, interpreting its emotional conflicts, and providing the objects specific to its evolving interests.

If this helping mode of child care has been in recent times over-enthusiastically advocated, even if not yet widely implemented, it may be because insufficient account has been taken of the complementary needs of adults which children must learn to understand if they and their elders are collectively to edge towards full psychosocial functioning.

It is not appropriate here to describe the various interlinked models of human development and functioning which have been propounded, such as those of Erikson, Freud, Maslow, Piaget, Bruner, Rogers, Kelly, Skinner and Kohlberg, nor indeed to chart the actual behaviours and needs of parents, such as have been executed so thoroughly by the Newsons and reviewed comprehensively by the Rapoports. Instead a number of recurring themes related to the parental task will be briefly mentioned, leaving many other accessible sources to fill in the detail.

Much of the literature on child care and development identifies a number of phases related normatively to chronological age. These phases are usually approximately divided as: babyhood (the first year of life), infancy (one to three), early childhood (three to six), childhood (six to twelve), adolescence (thirteen to eighteen), followed by early adulthood (eighteen plus). Each of these phases is characterised by clusters of physical, intellectual and social traits which give indications of the kinds of active parental and other caregiver responses which are likely to facilitate further development. But similar cues at different ages and with different children need differing interpretations. For example, exaggerated 'bragging' behaviour at four represents reality testing and the deciphering of the 'rules' of the social environment; at twelve it more likely reflects underlying feelings of social inadequacy. Temperament and personality variations also lead to varied signs which require individual understanding. In part at least we may reasonably speculate that parenthood will become more sensitive and effective if the rudiments of our knowledge of developmental psychology and individual variation can be consciously applied in everyday situations; but there are no unfailing recipes.

Parents influence their children's behaviour in many ways by providing:

1 stable bonds and relationships (including those between brothers and sisters) which can provide a basis for the child's growing circle of friends and acquaintances outside the family, and a comfort in times of distress;

2 models of behaviour in response to life events and stresses, and which may be copied not necessarily consciously but at the periphery of awareness;

3 a range of attitudes and values which may be adhered to or,

particularly in adolescence, rebelled against;

4 the raw materials of life, not simply shelter, food and clothing, but language, music and other ranges of symbolic and aesthetic expression, and books, toys and other tools for enjoyment, play, making, exploring and responding to the environment; and

5 selective encouragement or discouragement of particular behaviours within a framework of discipline.

Through these means, along with others from school, media and community, the child develops his expectations, ideas, standards and character. In order to provide these means parents need:

(a) knowledge in interaction with experience, if their actions are to be considered, in the sense of being thought through; and

(b) certain minimal permitting circumstances, including adequate income, housing, self-knowledge, self-esteem and feelings of well-being with respect to other people.

The eventual transition of dependent child to autonomous adult stands the chance of being least painful, amid the inevitable and natural minor crises of growth, if the home has been stable and responsive to, and understanding of each member's needs. Real individual freedoms are born from genuine and loving security. With regard to such foundation principles, the issues raised by the concept of social class are to some degree irrelevant, for although differences in rearing practices, such as feeding, discipline, and consonance with school norms, have been charted, it is neither a helpful nor a justified step to evaluate these comparatively. Similar considerations apply to many of the rearing practices of other ethnic groups, for beyond nutrition and basic child care principles, lack of knowledge and understanding of effects of the behaviour of whole-family networks in natural environments imposes severe restrictions upon definitive and prescriptive advice.

Before concluding this chapter on the tasks of parenthood within the family context, it is appropriate and important to mention that the nature and behaviour of the child controls to some extent the responses of the parents. This is of course particularly evident in the case of children with obvious physical or mental handicap. The relationships between parents and children are bidirectional, reciprocal, interacting and mutually regulating. Parents from the moment of birth can never be in total control of, nor accountable for their children's behaviour. The human organism is not infinitely malleable by the environment, as we noted in the discussion of genetic endowment in the previous chapter. Likewise, the most skilled, motivated and highly informed parent will make 'mistakes' in parenthood, as patterns of behaviour are misunderstood; everyone has limits of parental performance. Parents, like teachers, are human and fallible. Most children accommodate parental misjudgments provided that they sense an underlying love, security and considered purpose; fortunately, too, some of the more serious errors of parental judgment, as perceived by the child, may be resolved at a later stage of life cycle development of parent and child if bridges of communication have been left sufficiently intact during and after a crisis period.

Nevertheless, parenthood is demanding, and at times infinitely testing of the adult character, and we need to make sure that our social and educational arrangements allow it to remain both feasible and rewarding.

We have found no better way to raise a child than to reinforce the ability of his parent(s), whether natural or substitute, to do so.

The Court Report (1976)

Over 30 years ago Richard Titmuss pointed out that we had always assumed that the family was fundamental to our social structure, had taken it for granted and never really acted as though we appreciated it, so that its importance and effectiveness had become eroded, not wilfully, but by neglect. It is no small irony that our discovery of the special states and needs of childhood has happened at a time when, as we shall see in the next chapter, social forces seem to be undermining at least some of the familial foundations upon which responsibility has rested for supporting them and encouraging their development.

## References

ALDOUS, J. (1978). *Family Careers and Developmental Change in Families*. New York: John Wiley.

BARNARD, J. (1975). *The Future of Parenthood: The New Role of Mothers*. Open Forum series. London: Calder and Boyars.

BANNISTER, D., and FRANSELLA, F. (1971). *Inquiring Man*. Harmondsworth: Penguin Books.

BOWLBY, J. (1979). *The Making and Breaking of Affectional Bonds*. London: Tavistock Publications.

de MAUSE, L. (ed.) (1976). *The History of Childhood*. London: Souvenir Press.

ERIKSON, E. (1965). *Childhood and Society*. Harmondsworth: Penguin Books.

FARMER, M. (1979). *The Family*. Harlow: Longman.

GEORGE, V., and WILDING, P. (1972). *Motherless Families*. London: Routledge and Kegan Paul.

GORER, G. (1973). *Sex and Marriage in England Today*. St Albans: Panther Books.

GREEN, M. (1976). *Goodbye Father*. London: Routledge and Kegan Paul.

JOLLY, H. (1975). *Book of Child Care*. London: Allen and Unwin.

KAY, F. G. (1972). *The Family in Transition*. Newton Abbot: David and Charles.

KITZINGER, S. (1978). *Women as Mothers*. London: Collins Fontana.

LAKE, T., and HILLS, A. (1979). *Affairs: The Anatomy of Extra Marital Relationships*. London: Open Books.

LASLETT, P. (1971). *The World we have Lost*. London: Methuen.

LASLETT, P. (ed.) (1972). *Household and Family in Past Time*. London: Cambridge University Press.

LESLIE, G. R. (1979). *The Family in its Social Context*. Oxford: Oxford University Press.

NEWSON, J., and NEWSON, E., with BARNES, P. (1976). *Seven Years Old in the Home Environment*. London: Allen and Unwin.

NEWSON, J., and NEWSON, E. (1970). *Four Years Old in an Urban Community*. Harmondsworth: Penguin Books.

NEWSON, J., and NEWSON, E. (1971). *Patterns of Infant Care in an Urban Community*. Harmondsworth: Penguin Books.

SHORTER, E. (1976). *The Making of the Modern Family*. London: Collins.

VAUGHAN, V. C., and BRAZELTON, T. B. (1976). *The Family—Can it be Saved?* Chicago, Ill.: Year Book Medical Publishers.

WINNICOTT, D. W. (1957). *The Child and the Family*. London: Tavistock Publications.

# CHAPTER 4

# Social Indicators Relevant to Child Care

Having illuminated how important home is in promoting educational achievement, and having described, albeit briefly, the magnitude and complexity of the conscientious parent's task in modern society with respect to child care within the family, we now turn to a range of data (mostly from official sources) which reflect something of how the present-day families in the UK, and the children within them, are faring, and the directions in which changes are moving. We shall look at parental work patterns, at the divorce rate, at the number of one-parent families, at children 'in care', at illegitimacy, abortion and venereal disease, at maternal depression, infant mortality and non-accidental child injuries, and at truancy, juvenile delinquency and drug abuse. We will see that most of these social indicators are pointing in the wrong direction as far as effective child care is concerned. Whilst no single indicator is a reliable index of society's capacity for coping with children's needs and interests, the collective data can be regarded as pointing to a need for extensive preventive action. Not only is such action justifiable in its own right, not least as a way of assisting the well-being of children, and before a family situation has reached crisis point, it would also serve to avert the collapse of the educational, social and medical services under overwhelming crisis case loads. Whether these trends in the way society is progressing are in total qualitatively or quantitatively worse or better than for former generations, though naturally a question of interest to child care historians, is to some degree irrelevant. Suffering children, or children and those who care for them at risk or already in difficulties, represent a recognisable social concern *now*.

For example, since 1972 the National Society for the Prevention of Cruelty to Children (the largest voluntary organisation in the UK concerned with child abuse of all kinds) has opened an average of about 18,000 new cases involving about 50,000 children each year. Of these cases the basic family circumstances are categorised by field staff approximately as:

| | |
|---|---|
| serious disharmony between parents | 25% |
| single parent families with specific needs | 30% |
| disturbed parent/child relations | 15% |
| physical, mental or emotional disability within family | 20% |
| financial or housing problem | 30% |

(Some families appear in more than one category, accounting for a total greater than 100%.)

Complacency cannot surely be the response of a caring society to these cases of revealed suffering. Nor can they be accounted for by individual psychosocial deficits, for everyone's individual behaviour is heavily conditioned by the moral, social and economic environment in which we live.


PATTERNS OF PARENTAL EMPLOYMENT

* Sandra the 25 year-old mother of two-year-old Trevor has to do factory work full-time because her husband is an inefficient provider and she has to take most of the financial responsibility of the household. Trevor has been looked after by a kindly neighbour, who is not registered as a child-minder, but she is moving from the district at the end of the week. A nursery school place is urgently required.

* Jenny is the 30-year-old wife of an insurance executive and mother of two primary school children. She has a full-time job fifteen miles from home and she has to leave home for work in her car an hour before school starts. Her husband leaves the two children with a neighbour when he sets off for his work a quarter of an hour later; he is often away overnight on business. The children let themselves into home on their return from school, and two hours later Jenny returns. The children each have £3 per week pocket money which is doubled in the school holidays.

The number of families with young children in which both parents go out to work has been increasing steadily in recent years. This reflects the growth of married women in employment outside the home generally, for since 1951 about 2 million women have been added to the workforce, and current projections suggest that a further 2 million females will be so added by 1986, if jobs are available. Approaching 50% of married women are now euphemistically referred to in the official figures as 'economically active', as if to underline the fact that those who exercise the skills of homemaking and child care do not engage in productive work which has economic benefits for the nation; this is about $2\frac{1}{2}$ times the 1951 level. Men it seems rarely respond to parenthood by reducing their work commitments since economic needs frequently demand more overtime.

Reliable figures on the proportion of married women with children aged less than sixteen who go out to work do not seem to be available; the Department of Employment does not keep records about the family status of the female workforce, for example. Some estimates can however be made from census and general household survey data (see Tables 1 to 3).

*Table 1*

*Mothers with pre-school age children*

|  | 1961 | 1971 | 1974 | 1976 |
|---|---|---|---|---|
| Number working | 333,500 | 588,600* | 750,000 (est) | 900,000 |
| % working | 11 | 20† | 26§ | 27‡ |

\* Almost one half of these worked more than 21 hours per week.
† Comparable figure for children aged 5 to 10 = 41%
  Comparabe figure for children aged 11 to 15 = 52%.
‡ Comparable figure for children aged 5 to 15 = 65%
§ Two local studies of Inner London areas in 1975 both found 24% of children under the age of one with employed mothers.

Thus in the late 1970s it would appear that about 40% of women with children of school or pre-school age go out to work. The 1976 General Household Survey suggested that approximately one in every three mothers did so on a full-time basis, though the increase in part-time working trends seems greater over recent years. Nevertheless, there are about six children under five whose mothers work more than 30 hours per week for every full-time day nursery place available, and the registered child-minding system still leaves half of such children uncatered for.

The positive benefits to the nation of these employment patterns (second only to Denmark of countries within the European Economic

*Table 2*

*Economically active married women with children (as % of the total of married women working)*

| Years married | | 1951 | 1961 | 1971 |
|---|---|---|---|---|
| 0 | | 10.7 | 11.4 | 13.5 |
| 1 | | 10.2 | 11.7 | 14.7 |
| 2 | | 11.2 | 12.6 | 16.1 |
| 3 | | 11.7 | 12.9 | 16.8 |
| 4 | | 12.3 | 12.4 | 17.6 |
| 5 | ↑Likely to have pre-school age children | 12.6 | 13.3 | 19.3 |
| 6 | dren | 13.9 | 13.9 | 21.8 |
| 7 | Likely to have primary school | 14.9 | 15.8 | 25.1 |
| 8 | ↓children | 15.7 | 17.3 | 29.1 |
| 9 | | 17.1 | 20.6 | 32.5 |

*Table 3*

*% Working mothers, 1971, according to number of dependent children*

| Dependent children | % Mothers working |
|---|---|
| 1 | 43.2 |
| 2 | 38.7 |
| 3 | 35.1 |
| 4 | 30.8 |
| 5 or more | 26.8 |

Community) should not be underestimated in terms of keeping the wheels of the industrial and services machines moving, but since relatively few couples exchange their traditional roles, with father staying with the children as homemaker, the pattern results in less parental *time* being available for child care. Also adequate substitutes, formerly more widely available through the extended family and close neighbours, are far from easy to find. Of course, as was mentioned in the previous chapter, time for the parental task is not the only consideration; the quality and intensity of the interaction between parents and children is most important. Nevertheless, finite time and fresh energy is required for the task of effective child-rearing. Overtired parents never free from the strains of employment, travel to and from work, and then shopping, housework and child care, must find their responsibilities at times overwhelming, putting strains on the whole network of family relationships.

A figure significantly related to patterns of family employment is the number of so-called 'latchkey children'. Again reliable figures are hard to come by, but it has been estimated that over half a million children aged five to fifteen are left alone for longish periods after school, and during the school holidays the number could be about one-third higher. While the number of hours worked by mothers on a part-time basis may be no more than the hours children spend in school, working hours at the place of employment and school hours rarely coincide, so that problems of journeys home from school and opening the house remain for many young children even in those cases. The increased provision of holiday play schemes for school children (now due for reappraisal after  recent public expenditure cuts) may have been outpaced by the tendency of more parentcouples to work.

The consequences for children of the absence of adult care for significant periods of the day are probably far-reaching. There is on the one hand the loneliness and depression of those who act according to their parents' wishes and return to the empty home, and on the other increased vandalism and other forms of juvenile delinquency and truancy (see pages 52–4) resulting from unconforming youngsters with the problem of too much unsupervised time on their hands. Simple common sense would suggest that at least some of the 24,000 road accidents to pedestrians aged five to fourteen during 1976 might have been avoided by a combination of changes in work patterns and after school and holiday provision.

Over the next two decades we are however likely to see major changes in recent patterns of family employment, as Britain grapples with the huge problems of structural unemployment caused by technological innovation, legislation, public expenditure cuts and variations in patterns of world trade. The notion of democratic work sharing using the family as a resource unit for policy is discussed in Chapter 6 (page 109) as a means whereby traditional unemployment figures may be contained, while at the same time more firmly guaranteeing the care of children by their parents.

THE STABILITY OF FAMILIES: TRENDS IN DIVORCE

During this century the divorce rate has increased by well over a hundred-fold to 9.5% of married couples per year, though because of the increase in longevity, the duration of married life expectancy has doubled in the same period. Figure 4 shows that the number of divorces is still increasing, though the trend seems more settled after the large movements of 1970 to 1972 following the passing of the Divorce Law Reform Act in 1969 (consolidated 1973) which extended the grounds to include two years' separation with the consent of both parties, and five years' separation where one party witholds consent.

This trend of increasing levels of divorce is common to all Western countries, and no doubt in many cases results in a greater corporate happiness, for people rightly have greater expectations of marriage in terms of personal fulfilment than they once did; in particular, women (who in 1976 and 1977 filed 70% of divorce petitions) seem prepared to tolerate less than formerly. Divorce is therefore presently an essential safety valve for communities which do little to provide preventive help by way of preparation for marriage. Another view of the size of the 'safety valve' is that in the 1970s there has been one divorce for every three weddings.

Here however we are concerned more specifically with the effects of divorce on children, for they are involved in three-quarters of divorce cases. Table 4 shows the numbers of children aged up to sixteen recently involved in parental divorce, which affects approaching 80,000 families per year. Each child presently being born has therefore about a 1 in 3.5 chance of being caught up in parental divorce before leaving school.

The divorce statistics are naturally reflected in the numbers of one-parent families which have shown a 6% annual increase since 1971 despite the fact that remarriage is becoming increasingly popular. At

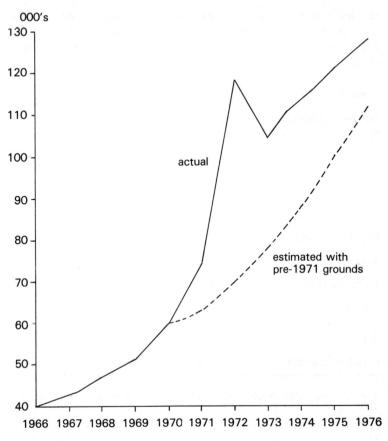

4 *Divorce (England and Wales) 1966–76*

*Table 4*

*Number of children under 16 affected by divorce (England and Wales)*

| Age of children | 1975 | 1976 | 1977 |
|---|---|---|---|
| 0 to 4 | 33,000 | 34,000 | 34,000 |
| 5 to 10 | 69,000 | 71,000 | 69,000 |
| 11 to 16 | 43,000 | 47,000 | 46,000 |
| Total up to 16 | 145,000 | 152,000 | 149,000 |

the time of writing, one family in nine with dependent children (11%) has only one parent; well over one million children have only one parent (see Table 5) with consequent stresses on both parent and children.

*Table 5*

*One-parent families*

| Type | 1971 | 1976 | % living alone with children |
|------|------|------|------------------------------|
| Divorced mothers | 120,000 | 230,000 | 76 |
| Separated mothers | 170,000 | 185,000 | 80 |
| Widows | 120,000 | 115,000 | 88 |
| Unmarried mothers | 90,000 | 130,000 | 44 |
| Lone fathers | 70,000 | 90,000 | 74 |
| Total | 570,000 | 750,000 | |
| Children affected | 1 million | 1.25 million | |

(Data from Population Trends 13, Autumn 1978; the 1971 figures are revised estimates.)

Nearly three quarters (74%) of the 750,000 one-parent families live alone with no other adult in the same household, and among lone mothers the same proportion (50%) go out to work as among married women with children in two parent families. The *time* available for child rearing in the one-parent family is therefore inevitably a precious yet scarce resource in view of the many other necessary demands on the lone parent.

The drain on the public purse of marriage breakdown is substantial, it being estimated that £5,000,000 per week is paid out in supplementary benefits to about a quarter of a million families who are unsupported after separation and divorce. The 1979 report of a Home Office working party which suggested a government 'minister for marriage' had at least some economic motivation, and it would be encouraging to see even a small fraction of these costs of breakdown going towards prevention; road safety is an appropriate analogy.

What data of this kind cannot portray is the cost in terms of human misery for both parents and children of such breakdowns in relationships, and data on significantly unhappy marriages which, for one reason or another, do not lead to divorce is unavailable. Despite the excellent work of marriage guidance counsellors, at present only about one quarter of potential cases at most are being seen by qualified personnel prior to decisions about termination.* With remarriage increasing dramatically (by 46% during 1971–5, so that now something over 30% of all marriages are remarriages), many children are living in new families with usually only one of their natural parents. Within these arrangements there are naturally potential benefits, for if bitterness can be overcome, new 'extended families' effectively emerge.

The effects of divorce or significant parental tension upon youngsters have hardly been adequately charted in terms of emotional stability, social confidence and educational performance. School attainment, expressed as mathematics and reading scores, did not appear significantly lower for children of one-parent families compared with those having two parents in a recent examination of the National Child Development Study data when other factors, especially family income, were taken into account. Michael Rutter's studies have shown that behavioural disturbance in children is strongly associated with family discord and disorder, with boys being much more immediately susceptible to ill-effects than girls. However, children who are reared in discordant quarrelsome homes are more likely to be protected if they have a good relationship with one parent (either father or mother) and/or they move to a happier home situation. These modifying factors do not heal the wounds to the child, but they can considerably ameliorate them. Marriages lacking in warmth, but in which there is no overt discord or hostility, do not seem to increase the chances of child disturbance, so there may well be some wisdom in the old adage 'be careful what you say in front of the children'; however, that is for many couples in tension far easier said than done.

While clearly most children 'survive' the trauma of divorce, and

* The National Marriage Guidance Council conducted about 152,000 interviews on 33,000 cases in 1977; of these 28,500 cases were new, and although there was a three-fold rise in the number of cases which involved counselling both partners compared with 1972, this category was but 30% of the total.

many find themselves in happier, less stressful new family situations with at least one strong bond with a natural parent, the underlying and subtle effects are hard for research to unravel. Children of divorced parents report feeling 'used' during and after divorce, and see the act of divorce increasing the emotional distance between them and particularly their fathers. Although children's experience of divorce leads to less confidence regarding their own ability to attain married happiness, and perhaps to develop parenting skills (for psycho-analytic work has suggested that much marital conflict arises from un-resolved conflicts in childhood), a romantic view of a Utopian union seems to survive even the most disturbing and devastating experiences of human relationships. The need for loving, accepting and warm companionship is seemingly deeply engrained in most of us; a crucial question rests in whether the abilities required to foster this can be developed on a wider scale through teaching and sensitively executed educational experience.

CHILDREN IN CARE

In a very real sense of course *all* children are, or should be, 'in care', but an increasing number are having to be cared for with little direct involvement of their parents through local authorities and voluntary agencies. Despite the rapidly declining birth-rate (25% reduction between 1970 and 1975) there has been a continuous rise (amounting to about 15%) of cases in local authority care during the 1970s. Approaching 120,000 children are now so placed in the UK at a possible yearly cost to the nation of £500 million. Most of these children are in care through no fault of their own; that is, they are not delinquent but have suffered parental death or illness, or have inadequate home conditions, or they have been deserted or battered by one or both parents.

It has never been easy for the care agencies to provide adequate long-term substitutes for parents within an institutional setting, and even today only 14% of residential care staff have formal training. Not that training can provide that spark of unconditional love which any child needs; yet nonetheless with the age distribution of children in care rising steadily, the range of care staff skills required in many settings is enormous, and too few of the community seem presently 'called' to give the necessary long-term service. The more recent emphases of agencies, including the National Children's Home, upon family-based support is a well understood response to social and economic reality.


ILLEGITIMACY, ABORTION AND VENEREAL DISEASE

* Despite the increased availability of contraceptives, family planning advice and other health education efforts, about one in six live births are conceived outside marriage, and in only about half of these cases does marriage between the partners result.

* Abortions in the UK, though only one half of the rate per 1000 women of childbearing age compared with the USA, are still being executed at a rate of over 2000 per week, i.e. about one for every five live births. In 1974, when a stable abortion rate had been reached subsequent to the change in legislation, almost 25,000 abortions were performed on females aged sixteen to nineteen, with a further 3335 for the eleven to fifteen age group. Over half the abortions are for single women.

* Venereal disease, especially gonorrhoea, is far from being contained, and over the years 1966 to 1974, among the under nineteens it doubled for males and trebled for females.

Such statistics, reflecting sexual practices and something of the concern people have for one another, may of themselves have little direct bearing upon early child care, though they do embody a good deal of personal distress and grief for many of those centrally involved, who include a significant proportion of teenagers. More important, however, is the underlying ethic which assumes that the personal and social costs of free experimentation are insignificant compared with the alleged benefits, even where potentially viable human life is concerned. The prevalence of such an ethic must have some impact upon our total attitudes to human care. Sex-related problems and behaviour extend far beyond their surface physiological dimensions and are a crucial component of our psychological identity. While the majority of us are shielded, perhaps fortunately, from the vision of a writhing viable foetus aborted after the twentieth week of pregnancy, we cannot escape our moral complicity in such events. A text about child care cannot avoid at least some mention of foetal care, though this is not the place to discuss the point at which the foetus becomes a child.

MATERNAL DEPRESSION

* Phyllis has two pre-school age children. She lives on the seventh floor of a block of high rise flats, gets depressed and lonely and cannot get up in the morning. The children are very lively and often play around the nearby shops on their own.

* Veronica longs to return to her work as a medical secretary but her husband and mother have always believed that she should be with her two young children at least until they reach school age. She finds the children basically a chore rather than a stimulant, and she leaves them regularly with neighbours while she goes to the squash and tennis club.

A number of relatively recent community studies of mothers of pre-school children indicate that around 40% suffer from significant distress and depression, though there are probably quite large differences between geographical areas. The majority of such women seem not to seek medical help. Variables related to maternal depression include housing problems and social isolation; satisfaction with the daily home environment in terms of its suitability for both mother and child seems to weigh heavily on levels of maternal stress, and income level is here a related factor. The absence of confiding intimate relationships with husband or relative or friend also seems important. It has been suggested that benefits gained by working mothers are that they are able to meet more people and to have a greater sense of self-esteem through feeling valuable *outside* the home. This is no doubt true in a proportion of cases, but presupposes that a mother's experience of employment is happy, and that workmates provide the necessary confidential intimacy, both of which seem doubtful in many work situations.

Women with pre-school children who have conflicting feelings about being full-time mothers and housewives, that is having a feeling of duty to stay at home but being dissatisfied with the role and wanting employment, are about four times as likely to be prescribed sedatives and tranquillizers as those who experience no such conflict. If, as seems likely, the labour market demand for women with children declines over the next few years despite the equal opportunities legislation, then means must be found of making women's home lives more socially, and probably economically, rewarding if dissatisfaction with their state and the consequent halo effects on their children are to be avoided.

INFANT MORTALITY

In the 1950s Britain had significantly lower infant mortality statistics than, for example, Japan and France. While infant mortality has continuously declined in all countries of the developed world since the 1939–45 war, the fall in Britain is less pronounced than for many other nations. Table 6 presents a brief selection of the data.

*Table 6*

*Infant mortality (expressed as deaths under one year old for every 1000 live births)*

| Country | 1965 | 1973 | 1977 |
|---------|------|------|------|
| England and Wales | 19.0 | 16.3 | 15.4 |
| Scotland | 23.1 | 19.0 | 15.8 |
| France | 21.9 | 15.5 | 11.4 |
| Denmark | 18.7 | 11.5 | 8.7 |
| Sweden | 13.3 | 9.9 | 8.0 |
| Japan | 18.5 | 11.3 | 8.9 |

There are wide regional variations within Britain for this indicator of the early health care of infants, while for every early death two infants survive with permanent handicaps. A wide range of factors is involved in the incidence and prevention of infant mortality, but few can seriously doubt that more systematic preventive efforts could have an impact. For example, only about 20% of British mothers seek ante-natal care during the first three months of pregnancy, even though it is well known that early reporting is crucial for the diagnosis of potential foetal deficits. There is a high correlation between the incidence of low birth weight babies and clinic defaulting mothers. In Britain, unlike in Sweden, for example, the social conditioning encouraging mothers-to-be to make full use of the available services has not yet fully taken place. Relations, husbands and boyfriends have a duty to encourage the use of these services, and might do so if they were adequately informed. Programmes of school-based immunisation of adolescent females against rubella (German measles) could reduce the number of cases of foetal deformity, while at the same time raising community awareness regarding responsible preparation for the baby.

In France a legal measure introduced in 1975, requiring at least six pre-natal and post-natal clinic check-ups in order for mothers to qualify for the periodical social security benefits, has vastly reduced perinatal mortality to about 40% of the UK level for comparable demographic regions. Failing to take the three-month ante-natal check-up means that the French mother forfeits the equivalent of £40, the six-month forfeit is £80, and the two-year post-natal (with toddler) £60. The French clearly believe that these strong measures are likely to involve much less social cost than the subsequent care of children with possibly avoidable handicaps, but it takes bold policy to invest in prevention using such incentives. In Britain a mother may collect the miserly single £25 maternity grant (last fixed in 1969) from the 26th week of pregnancy.

NON-ACCIDENTAL INJURY TO CHILDREN

* 'I lock myself in the lavatory to cage in my violence towards the child.'

* 'I was often violent, and although she was often bruised I always managed to stop before anything was actually broken. I felt very ashamed and guilty and I didn't know why I should beat the baby instead of just loving it. I was too frightened to tell anyone, even my husband.'

* 'My second baby was a holy horror and but for my husband he would have been a statistic.'

* 'I spanked them a lot for the least little thing, yet I loved them dearly and dressed them well. So why was I so cruel?'

The haunted confusion of four mothers, unknown on the baby battering risk registers of social workers, is starkly conveyed in their own words prompted by the unconventional preventive efforts of 'Parents Helpline' and 'Child Care Switch-board' (see Appendix 2, pages 152–3).

Every week in Britain two very young children are battered to death and perhaps about one thousand sustain non-fatal injuries inflicted upon them by their parents. The British Paediatric Association estimates that this kind of violence within the home is the fourth commonest cause of death in the first five years of life. About 400 cases of non-accidental brain injury to children in the first year of life are diagnosed each year, often with visual impairment. In this field hard evidence is difficult to gather, but the Royal College of Psychiatrists estimate 300 deaths, 3000 serious injuries and 40,000 minor injuries per year for the UK—a problem grave enough for government enquiries and a recent White Paper, *Violence to Children* (HMSO Cmnd 7123, March 1978).

Violence within the family setting is not new, though the general public and the professions have become increasingly conscious of the problem, both as it affects wives and as it affects children. While frequently earlier identification of children at serious risk is now possible, many tragic cases slip through the net of care; Maria Colwell was known across the nation in 1975–6, yet many others suffer without any such publicity. The risk of non-accidental violence decreases as children become older, for feeding, sleeping and crying problems seem to be the major parental irritants. A number of young children also inflict injury upon themselves when they cannot cope with suffering the loss of a beloved person, either in or close to their families, or, for example, whilst in residential care: the desire for self-destruction can be the culmination of uncontained personal stress.

Family violence, as one might expect, is often associated with a range of other stresses, such as illegitimacy, premature birth, irregular employment, criminal records, and psychiatric disorder. A recent study found that over one third of mothers who were violent to their children had suffered violence in their own childhood, which is an example of another cycle of disadvantage, that of replicated patterns of behaviour. Yet the problem is not simply one of individual behaviour since, as the Court Report (1976) noted, one could expect that in a healthy society child battering would happen only in rare pathological cases. Perhaps more vividly than in any other sphere these occurrences illustrate some of the stressful family dimensions of child care today. Children whose behaviour patterns appear least malleable act as a stimulant for uncontrolled rage, and parents need to be able to find means of physical and psychological escape from the severe irritations of their offspring. Psychological relief through the sharing of parental burdens with others has proved a valuable preventive step in many cases.

The promotion of self-knowledge among parents of their propensities for aggression towards their children and of a range of avoidance strategies is possible within parent education programmes. The recognition that in many cases negative feelings towards children are normal for parents from time to time can help remove guilt and prevent extreme parental reaction.

JUVENILE DELINQUENCY, DRUG ABUSE AND MENTAL DISORDER

For many years now there have been significant increases in the rates of juvenile delinquency. Although girls are only about one fifth as likely to commit an indictable offence as boys, since about 1963 the rate of incidence of crime among girls has trebled compared with a doubling in the case of boys. The peak age for juvenile delinquency has remained quite steady over the years at fourteen to fifteen. Among boys aged fourteen to sixteen about one in twelve of the population were found guilty of or cautioned for indictable offences in 1977, when almost 200,000 cases among ten to sixteen-year-olds were examined in England and Wales.

While clearly there are multiple factors affecting juvenile misconduct, the experience of the police and probation services is that the child from a caring home, though not necessarily an affluent one, is less likely than one from a negligent one to be at risk of breaking the law, and more likely to respond to remedial treatment upon conviction. At least some crime has its origins in emotional needs and aspirations, and in the quest for *attention* from someone, police and probation officers frequently find themselves acting as temporary substitute parents. The adolescent in particular requires the family unit to act as a stabilising feature during the sometimes tortuous transition to adulthood.

To be in possession of certain drugs is an indictable offence and leads to a good deal of concealment among adolescents. Studies show that most cases of drug abuse tend to begin in middle to late adolescence and often occur in situations where there is a history of emotional deprivation, disturbance and separation in the family. Although the number of notified narcotic addicts under the age of twenty fell during the early 1970s, the total number of misusers of drugs for which notification is not mandatory is very difficult to estimate. In terms of reported overdose cases the number appears to be rising, with a peak risk age of around twenty. While these problems for the community are related to the readier availability of the so-called 'soft' drugs in particular, and the practices of prescription by doctors and pharmacists, the need to experiment dangerously and then abuse the self originates from problems of emotional security and lack of purpose, which in many cases can be traced back to home experiences. The excessive consumption of alcohol among young people is also increasing and causing health educators considerable concern. While drinking and smoking habits derive largely from general societal attitudes upon which peers and the media have influence, the family context is also crucial in the development of such health related habits.

The statistics of psychiatric disorders in children and young people are very inadequately charted, but between 1964 and 1973 there was a 25% increase in out-patient referrals to the child guidance and psychiatric services, and medical opinion strongly suggests that much mental disturbance is going undetected and untreated. The rise in depressive disorders in adolescence is reflected in the rising incidence of suicide, attempted suicide and the seeking of Samaritan help amongst youngsters; among adolescents it is estimated that there are 50 attempted suicides for every successful one. Between 5% and 10% of children are currently believed by the medical profession to have mental disorders of sufficient severity to handicap them in their everyday lives. Such disorders are again attributable to a complex interplay of factors both within the child and between him and his psychological and social circumstances. Adolescent boys from discordant families, with a history of mental problems and living in metropolitan areas are those at most risk. Home, and to a larger extent school, both have real opportunities to promote mental health, and as far as school is concerned this objective could be taken more seriously in professional discussions which seek to balance the whole curriculum, and to set up appropriate counselling rather than simply careers guidance services.

TRUANCY AND INDISCIPLINE

A number of researches have indicated that school truancy and indiscipline are increasing. For example, the prolonged truancy rate in Glasgow secondary schools almost doubled between 1964 and 1975, and is now estimated, as in Sheffield, at something over 2%. A recent Scottish national survey (executed in 1976 for the Pack Report) discovered that over 3% of total pupil school time was lost by truancy, which is equivalent to some 22% of all absences. Over the six-week period of this survey of twelve to sixteen-year-olds, over 15% of all children were absent from school without adequate explanation, and for the final year at school it appeared that a quarter of both boys and

girls played truant. The most recent national figures for England and
Wales (1974) seem broadly comparable.

Although truancy, like the rest of the social indicators here
chronicled, has multiple causes, including factors for which the schools
must be held responsible, such as inappropriate curricular experiences
through which children may be made to feel inadequate, the Pack
Report concluded that: 'There seems little doubt that family circumstances play the major role in cases of chronic truancy.' Some
parents do not discourage truancy, but the majority are either
unaware that their children are playing truant (for instance where
they are out at work during school hours), or there are family
difficulties such as marital disharmony which prevent regular school
attendance. Parents unable to cope with the problems of their own
lives, with family budgeting, with medical setbacks, and with little
insight into their children's needs, perhaps find it hard to summon up
enough energy and authority to urge their recalcitrant children to go
to school.

Indiscipline at school is even more difficult to chart than truancy,
but it is clear that teachers are having to cope with a significant range
of stressful incidents which arise from the failure of parents and other
adults to develop in children in their early years an adequate degree of
self-control and discipline regarding such matters as rudeness, violent
emotions, desire for possessions, respect of property and personal
hygiene. These problems seem to be increasing, and present schools
with many problems which lie outside the formal curriculum. Most
local authorities now have special units for disruptive pupils within
which the aim is to seek to promote eventual rehabilitation to normal
classes. However, these units can only cope with the most severe cases,
still leaving many problems inside ordinary classroom settings.

No teacher or school system can be expected to cope with all the
behavioural problems resulting from inadequate parental care. On
top of the perennial problems which schools face in providing basic
instruction in the normal school subjects and the customary pastoral
care of their pupils, the average class of 30 children in our ordinary, not
special, schools today contains pupils potentially at risk as estimated in
Table 7.

There are thus more than enough of these unsettling features for
each child in a class to carry on average at least one. There is also a
daunting array of possible background factors for teachers to consider
in evaluating a child's present behaviour in school and to act ap-

*Table 7*

*Social factors relating to a hypothetical 'average' class of 30 schoolchildren*

| *Idealised child care at possible risk through* | *Number affected* |
| --- | --- |
| Father unemployed | 1.5 |
| Mother out to work | 13 |
| Lone-parent family | 2 |
| In the throes of divorce | 0.4 |
| Of at least one divorced parent | 3 rising to 9 |
| In local authority/voluntary agency care | 0.3 |
| Delinquent this year | 0.7 |
| Born illegitimate | 3 |
| Pre-maritally conceived | 2 |
| One parent chronically sick | 2.5 |
| Moving house and home per year | 2.5 |

propriately. To distinguish healthy high spirits or naturally shy withdrawal from more deep-seated psychosocial disorder is by no means easy amid the multiple demands of the school day. In many instances, society is requiring the ideal teacher's role to be stretched wider than may be educationally desirable, let alone humanly possible. Certainly no teacher can expect that assumed norms of family life apply to the majority of children at school. The concepts of 'children at risk', or 'disadvantaged', traditionally implying minority phenomena, might well now need forgetting in professional discussion, to be replaced by the less prevalent 'bonuses', 'credits' or 'advantages' for children for securing their greatest educational achievement and life adjustment.

INDICATORS NOT CAUSES

It may be objected that throughout this chapter several 'non-standard' features of family life have been assumed to constitute items of potential handicap as far as child care is concerned. In many areas the necessary research has not been executed to prove causal relationships, and therefore we are left to interpret probabilities which may arise from these social indicators, deliberately labelled in the summarising Table 7 as possible factors through which the idealised loving security which should surround children may be at risk.

Treasury advisers in taking the 'temperature' of the national economy do not rely on a single index, be it the balance of trade, unemployment, or the gold and currency reserves. The national economy, like the weather, is an entity affected by a large number of variables whose interaction is complex and ever-changing. Assessing the health of the nation's family life, child care, and its educational systems presents researchers and advisory pundits with similar, and probably much more daunting, tasks. Yet social and educational policy cannot await all the refinements in research technique and data collection which may one day give us the desired insights into the mechanisms of complex social processes which are necessary for truly scholarly intervention. So notwithstanding the fact that we need more researches which are designed to study causal mechanisms, we must meanwhile take note of the range of social indicators which are available to us, and do our best to extrapolate intelligent action from them if we discover cause for concern regarding the fulfilment of human rights for both children and their parents.

While some of the data, especially when taken in sectional isolation, may be open to alternative interpretations, it has not been selected for presentation with any conscious bias; indeed much of it when unearthed from the public records seemed surprising. These statistical snapshots, reflecting at their base something of the way people treat each other, alarm at least this author. Collectively the data seem suggestive of deep afflictions affecting the children and families of our nation. The trends outlined have placed increasing, and now perhaps overwhelming, burdens on the social, educational and medical services. The fabric of much family life in the community seems insecure and tenuous, as the help of the extended family living only round the corner and effective community support are often eroded by changes in patterns of employment, housing and leisure.

In these developing circumstances, to which indifference to and inaction on the range of data can hardly be our response, the question needs to be posed:

'*Who* can be relied upon to provide long-term secure loving care to the children whom men and women can now, more than ever before, make a decision to produce?'

In fact, who cares enough for children, who have no political voice which can be heard?

Clearly, in a complex society such as our own, no single answer to these questions is possible, for parents and families are not able to act autonomously and unilaterally, independent of the constraints of policies worked out at national and local government levels. Voluntary societies, churches and other charities are similarly and probably appropriately constrained by the blessings and inertia of the 'democratic' process. But a range of interventions is now surely necessary for an improved quality of family life.

In the next chapter we look at possible long term preventive educational interventions in some detail, leaving an account of these within a wider range of social policies for families until Chapter 6.

## References

ANTHONY, E. J., and KOUPERNIK, C. (eds.) (1974). *The Child in his Family: Children at Psychiatric Risk*. New York: John Wiley.

COMBER, L. C., and WHITFIELD, R. C. (1979). *Action on Indiscipline*. Birmingham: National Association of Schoolmasters/Union of Women Teachers.

DUNNELL, K. (1979). *Family Formation 1976*. London: HMSO.

FERRI, E. (1976). *Growing Up in a One-Parent Family*. Slough: NFER Publishing.

FERRI, E., and ROBINSON, H. (1976). *Coping Alone*. Slough: NFER Publishing.

HOME OFFICE (1979). *Marriage Matters*. London: HMSO.

JONES, R. (1978). *How goes Christian Marriage?* London: Epworth Press.

ORDER OF CHRISTIAN UNITY (1979). *Torn Lives: The Effects of Divorce and the Law of Divorce on Children*. Becket Publications.

SCOTTISH EDUCATION DEPARTMENT (1977). *Truancy and Indiscipline in Schools in Scotland* (The Pack Report) London: HMSO.

| Education for Parenthood

*There is a marked contrast between the medical care given to a mother on the one hand, and the lack of effort on the other hand to prepare her and the father for the role they will want to play to give their child a good chance to mature fully.*

Sir Keith Joseph (1972)

Consider some observations of an experienced pre-school worker:

* Late speech development is present in about 50% of the children who come to our family centre. It is frequently related to disturbed emotional life at home, and is present in a large number of children of average or above average intelligence.

* Many of our mothers are unable to control their children without shouting or physical restraint. They do not attempt to contain their children's frustrations by the exercise of patient love, by alternative distraction or satisfaction, or by explanation. Such lack of understanding practices often leads to inappropriate over-confidence, such as the child having no sense of danger, or to a lack of confidence in which the child is frightened of facing yet one more new experience alone without a parent.

* There is an almost total ignorance amongst our parents of the normal stages of child development under the age of five. For example, a six-month-old child cannot be expected to obey an instruction to sit still in a chair, and, at nine months, baby is not ready simply to play with other children in the absence of parents.

* The majority of our mothers do not appreciate the relationship between the nature of the emotional bond they have with their children and their ability to teach and to control them. This

frequently expresses itself as an unwillingness to give patient attention to their children of the kind which we try to provide, and through which they learn, sometimes with the envy of the parents.

* There is a total lack of recognition of the importance and complexity of the child-rearing task. This appears to apply not only to the many deprived families with whom we work, but also to the many middle-class parents who ring up asking for child care placements for very young children to allow a professional mother to return to work within weeks of a child's birth.

* Parents frequently expect young children to take rapid and drastic changes in family dynamics in their stride with little emotional reaction.

* Many of our parents have great difficulty in maintaining adult relationships with any age group because they are quick to flare up and fall out with people once the other party ceases to meet their wishes in all respects. This same immature resenting attitude is often displayed towards their children when they do not meet the parents' ideas of how they should behave.

From a somewhat different perspective, Timothy Cook, Director of Family Service Units (FSU), a voluntary yet professional social work organisation operating 23 Units in most of the inner city areas in England, notes that education for parenthood amongst many of their multi-problem families has been almost non-existent. Although one of FSU's aims is to execute preventive work with such families, too often it is brought in when the chaos and stresses of the family are overwhelming; even endeavours through the schools are unlikely to have reached these parents, partly due to their earlier truancy, but also because the level and style of teaching and advice is likely to have been inappropriate.

TAKING PREVENTION SERIOUSLY

If we *really* care about children and their parents, some radical and massive interventions are surely necessary to reduce ignorance, to encourage sensitivity and responsibility, and to develop understanding, skills and confidence among parents and parents-to-be. The family is without doubt under pressure as a result of many social changes, but knowledgeable analysts on both sides of the Atlantic still believe that families in their various forms are crucial for children's well-being.

Families are and will continue to be the *first* line of support for children. We examined other alternatives to the family, and we didn't find any that we thought workable in our society.

Carnegie Council on Children (1977)

The family seems to be the most effective and economic system for fostering and sustaining the child's healthy development.

Urie Bronfenbrenner (1975)

Hence, although we are not concerned with propping up the family for its own sake, as if defending a somewhat useless accretion from the past, in essence we need to consider the historical, social and political *reality* that the family is not an outmoded institution. While it may be going through a painful period of transition, it yet remains a crucial, resilient and adaptable vehicle for delivering human concern and care for the majority, regardless of race or creed, and it can still be a bulwark amid the strains of living.

Thus if regardless of religious tradition or moral imperative, personal welfare depends upon living in ordinary families, and yet the family is besieged economically, legally, emotionally and socially, then the *prevention* of family and child welfare crises must begin with short and long-term *educational* initiatives on a scale hitherto unimagined. Teachers, social workers, residential care staff and their colleagues in other branches of the helping professions know that much human misery and dysfunction could be avoided if prevention were taken more seriously. Moreover they know that they can often do no more than give first aid to the case load of today—and even then many in real need slip through the overstretched net of care. Even if it were politically and economically possible to relieve all environmental stresses upon households (and that, as we will see in the next chapter, must be an aim of responsible government), there would remain interpersonal conflicts and inadequacies for which educational and therapeutic initiatives would still be necessary at parent and pre-parent levels. The 1979 Home Office report on marriage guidance summarises the case for continual support:

> The services for helping people with problems of relationships must keep pace with our increasingly complex society in which an expanding variety of options and greater freedom of choice are likely to increase the stress on the individual. Economic recovery

may facilitate the improvement of facilities, but it is unlikely to lessen the emotional problems of those who use them. Indeed material progress by itself often creates as many human problems as it solves.

Official government policy now includes a number of preventive and supportive objectives enshrined within accepted Select Committee recommendations reprinted in the White Paper *Violence to Children.* For example:

* The community at large should become much more aware of its responsibilities towards families with young children.

* The government, whether through the Department of Health and Social Security or the Department of Education and Science, should ensure that education for parenthood is available for boys and girls of all levels of intellectual ability.

* A determined effort should be made by health visitors and midwives in the ante-natal period to explain fully what life can be like with small children.

* Parents should be encouraged to form groups where parents who are at all anxious about the way in which they are bringing up their children can meet and preferably also provide some regular telephone service.

* More mother and toddler clubs should be established whether on a voluntary basis or publicly financed; and all parents should have access to such clubs. Day care facilities, such as nurseries and nursery schools, must be available to all parents and not just those who have succumbed to strain and been listed as social priorities.

It is to be hoped that these are neither shallow nor mere party-political words, but statements which can be translated into practice with enthusiasm over the coming years. They embody commitment to the concept of preparation and support for family responsibility, and this chapter is devoted to some analysis and description of what this might mean in educational terms within schools and further, higher and adult education. Taking prevention seriously in any sphere of potential human suffering means providing appropriate educational experiences and the necessary resources to undergird their potential impact.

THE CONCEPT OF 'PREPARING FOR FAMILY RESPONSIBILITY'

> *Future improvements in the health of children will depend as much on the beliefs and behaviour of parents as on the services provided.*
>
> The Court Report (1976)

Anyone wishing to search the literature in the field of 'preparation for parenthood' is faced with a somewhat daunting task due to ambiguities and inconsistencies of definition, and the number of professional fields and academic disciplines which seem relevant. Stern's pioneering and most useful international survey of the field two decades ago encountered this problem also and he felt obliged to give a note on terminology, while Sir Keith Joseph a little curiously found that 'preparation for parenthood' was a 'misleadingly narrow and confining title' when introducing the 1974 Department of Health and Social Security (DHSS) booklet on the subject.

In such a situation of inconsistency all an author can do is to draw a somewhat prescriptive map of the field which is in harmony with at least the bulk of the literature as it defines itself. Here the map being drawn is wide rather than narrow, for in some cases associated terms may mask rather more precise intentions; for example in Canada 'family life education' frequently equals sex education, and a 1974 UNESCO seminar on 'education for responsible parenthood' was essentially only about family planning.

Let us define *preparation for parenthood* as

> *those experiences incorporated in the education and training of young people which are relevant to the aim of helping them to become self-aware and to form stable relationships, so that in due course they may consider responsibly the possibilities of marriage, skilled parenthood and a fulfilled family life.*

Implicitly the assumption here is that 'preparation for parenthood' occurs at the pre-parent stage, although some of its legitimate content may be equally appropriate experience for existing parents.

Superficially at least it might seem that the concept 'preparation for parenthood' presumes acquiescence to social pressures which lead to automatic parenthood. Not so. If every child is to be a wanted child, then the responsibly considered rejection of the possibility of parenthood by couples is something to be encouraged, especially in a world already stretched in terms of resources by over-population. Preparation for parenthood courses should seek, among other things, to promote an awareness of what the long-term responsibility of having children involves, and whether that is compatible with the disposition, temperament and life goals of the individual and couple.

This kind of experience can thus assist people in deciding upon their real priorities, and a relatively child-free life-style ought to be considered as a respectable option open to all, though within a caring democracy certain socio-political obligations regarding the young are unavoidable, for everyone, whether or not they have children. Voluntary childlessness seems to be a growing feature among couples in both the USA* and Britain, and national organisations of non-parents now exist. The informal help which such couples can give with the care of other people's children could be significant, whether as aunts or uncles, or simply as good neighbours.

Let us further define *parent education,* in its specific sense as a subset of adult education, as:

> *any educational or related assistance for parents which contributes to the physical, mental and emotional care of their children, and of themselves in undertaking the parental role.*

Clearly such assistance provided after the onset of the parental role, or more strictly subsequent to the diagnosis of conception, will include the teaching and learning of *parentcraft,* that is skills and knowledge necessary for competent parental care in Western society (which may naturally also feature at pre-parent level). However, parent education will also be concerned with developing the personality of the parent, and with promoting and understanding of his or her total behaviour and attitudes in the family situation. The advancement of parent coping skills needs placing in this wider framework, for *the welfare of children can only be properly built upon an understanding of the total social and psychological welfare of their parents,* or those who choose to care for them.

The major topics of the field of Education for Parenthood (EFP) here being considered may be depicted pictorially by a Venn diagram (Figure 5, page 64) in which an *approximate* demarcation between the topics appropriate to each of the pre-parent and parenthood stages is indicated; however, many topics may clearly quite sensibly feature in either phase.

The context and foundation of this map rests in the reality of the corporate interdependence of family members, and of the consequent and changing responsibilities each has to the other. The clarification of these personal responsibilities through learning about the topics indicated is an essential goal of the field, and as such is necessarily a part of general *moral* education, yet with a relatively specific form of

* The US Census Bureau reported a fourfold increase over the years 1967 to 1973.

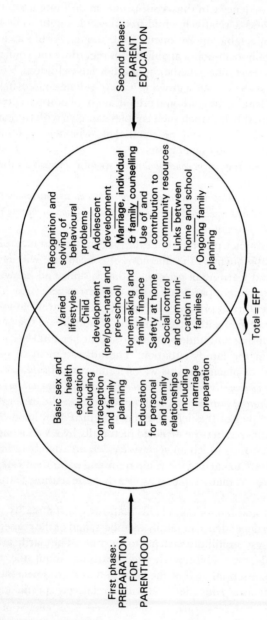

First phase:
PREPARATION
FOR
PARENTHOOD

Second phase:
PARENT
EDUCATION

Basic sex and health education including contraception and family planning

Education for personal and family relationships including marriage preparation

Varied lifestyles
Child development (pre/post-natal and pre-school)
Homemaking and family finance
Safety at home
Social control and communication in families

Recognition and solving of behavioural problems
Adolescent development
Marriage, individual & family counselling
Use of and contribution to community resources
Links between home and school
Ongoing family planning

Total = EFP

5   *A map depicting some of the major topics within Education for Parenthood (EFP). Topics shown within the overlapping area of the two circles may occur in either phase of EFP.*

social organisation as its focus, that is mother and/or father and children. The informative academic disciplines and practical crafts relevant to these topics are indicated in Figure 6.

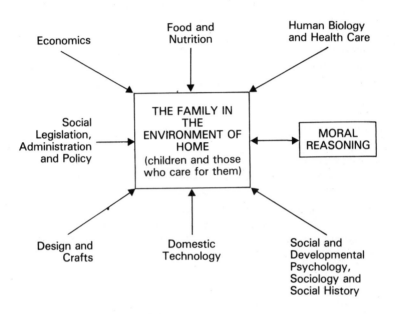

6   *Academic disciplines and practical crafts related to the exercise of parental responsibilities*

This diagram readily indicates both the breadth and complexity of education for parenthood. The complex pedagogical challenge of drawing these disciplines together for coherent experiences for parents and parents-to-be should not be underestimated. Effective topic-centred teaching which draws upon a range of academic and practical subjects is far more demanding than single discipline presentation, even though the topics may seem superficially to have more of an everyday connotation.

With our present lack of understanding of the detailed community needs within EFP it is premature to assign any weightings within or among the major topics shown in Figure 5 or the subject fields of Figure 6. As far as teaching approaches in relation to the definitions here presented are concerned, it is notable that some professionals have urged that the term 'preparation' rather than 'education' for parenthood should normally be used in order to impute more explicitly a wide range of teaching techniques. Apparently, for some, 'education' still seems to connote somewhat didactic teaching methods and passive, rather than activity-based, learning. This clearly need not be the case, and this text uses 'Education for Parenthood' as an inclusive term. A wide range of teaching and learning strategies seems very desirable in this field if abilities other than a knowledge of facts are to be fostered. Discussion groups, practical work, simulation, role play and so on will thus be used in many situations. Traditional educational methods will be likely to have limited application.

## EDUCATION FOR PARENTHOOD: AN OUTLINE OF ITS RECENT HISTORY

A crucial landmark within the highly diffuse EFP literature is undoubtedly Stern's international survey published in 1960. Stern provided a most useful history of developments in the field with particular emphasis on Germany, France, the USA and the UK, but unfortunately his work has never been updated. Much of what he pointed out with respect to the UK, however, remains fundamentally unchanged:

> In Great Britain parent education has been approached cautiously. There is no national organisation primarily responsible for it. There are no 'schools for parents', no 'schools for mothers', and the term 'parent education' is neither widely used nor even widely known . . . British experience illustrates an unfocalised, diffuse and informal approach.

Stern commented that internationally EFP had developed slowly, partly because of the widespread belief that parenting is a matter of instinct rather than learning, and partly because in the provision of school systems and public health and welfare services for children, governments had assumed that these would be able to make up for the deficits of home care. Parents had thus tended to become a blind spot in the eye of educational and social policy makers, and with the increasing professionalisation of the public services they remain to this day to some extent a 'nuisance' to teachers, medical and social staff. Arrays of experts having incrementally taken over parental responsibilities may indeed have caused the partial eclipse of parenthood in the so-called 'developed' world, thereby making it politically difficult to give EFP the serious consideration it is owed.

Since the availability of universal state education (from about 1870, in England and Wales), formal schooling has been expected to help realise a variety of social ambitions. It has been identified as a major means of achieving certain broad social aims which lie beyond the immediate experience of those pupils and students who are participating in it, and it is believed to have an important place in a network of cause/effect relationships in interaction with the wider society, even though, in the light of the discussion of Chapter 2, these may be somewhat more tenuous than traditionally imagined. The supposed relationships are focused politically in the substance of official enquiries and various kinds of educational and social advocacy, whether or not action ensues.

Although much social change through education has recently been concentrated upon institutional reform, such as the transition to comprehensive secondary education, reduced streaming of children according to perceived or measured abilities, the mooted integration of handicapped pupils into ordinary schools (the Warnock Report, 1978), and greater opportunities for access to further and higher education (albeit in part to trim the unemployment figures), a renewed faith in pedagogic and curricular reform to help bring about a greater degree of social justice and reconciliation has become evident during the 1970s. From visionaries of the last century, such as Matthew Arnold, onwards it has been recognised that social divisions are defined most crucially by cultural divisions derived from differential access to the cultural heritage, which comprises not simply knowledge and intellectual processes but also craft skills.

In the inter-war period there was a significant lobby for the concept of 'Education for Citizenship' which was seen as a form of social and political education, pursued across the school curriculum and promoting social order and responsibility. The stereotype of the good citizen was male:

> . . . consider what qualities a citizen of democracy should have in addition to the qualities that go to make a good father, a good scholar or a good businessman.
>
> Association for Education in Citizenship (1936)

Nonetheless it is interesting that 'fathering' as such was deemed to be important. An early publication of the post-war Ministry of Education located the family as the basic social unit responsible for the development of citizens able to work for the new 'good society'. Its role was described thus:

> The home is the first training ground of character, both individual

and social. It sets the first examples. It gives the first teaching. It is the first little community. Here justice—and injustice—are experienced for the first time.

*Citizens Growing Up* (HMSO, 1949)

This pamphlet proposed outline work for schools in 'homecraft', to involve 'parentcraft' as a component, and though there is brief mention of coeducational schemes, the primary responsibility for homemaking and the care of children is assumed to rest with the future mother:

> ... homecraft and parentcraft should be ... (available) ... for girls of every age in all types of schools.

Nonetheless, parenthood is seen as distinctive and as requiring appropriate social education, and this complemented a 1946 further education circular on homecraft from the central Ministry to Local Education Authorities (LEAs) which encouraged the initiation of appropriate courses. At about the same time an adviser in parentcraft was appointed to the Ministry of Health.

The LEAs, in whom curricular responsibility within their areas was firmly vested by the 1944 Education Act, have therefore had longstanding opportunities and encouragement to introduce appropriate EFP courses. Up to 1960 at least, as Stern noted, there seemed some reluctance:

> On the whole, preparation for family life in any organised form through schools has remained tentative beyond the mere practical aspects of housecraft ...

despite the fact that a survey of pupils' opinions executed around 1950 by Heron suggested that many adolescent boys and girls would welcome some kind of education for family life. Not surprisingly many of the respondents in Heron's survey had already had experience of looking after younger brothers and sisters, and he recommended that 'sex education' (then minimally present in most of the schools sampled) should be replaced by a wider based 'education for family life'. However, difficulties were anticipated because of 'the irrational resistance of many adults to the subject' and the 'dearth of suitable people to present the material'.

In the 1950s the identification of parenthood with motherhood was further reinforced by Bowlby's influential book *Child Care and the Growth of Love*, and it took until the early 1970s before some of the assumptions about specifically *maternal* deprivation were adequately questioned, even though the importance of environmental variables on the nature of child development which Bowlby demonstrated remain very significant, as we also saw in Chapter 2. However, the somewhat blind and holistic assumption of universally differentiated social roles of boys and girls in relation to their later parental obligations was implicit in the curricular discussions of the Crowther (1959) and Newsom (1963) Reports. One of the dangers of such an assumption is, of course, to suggest that the internal dynamics of family units, in which attributions and diagnosis may be identified, must *necessarily* be concerned with the differential sex roles which are enacted.

The Plowden Report *Children and their Primary Schools* (1967), which had the benefit of more research about the interdependence of home and school, offered guidelines on parent education through more formal home-school liaison, and although the consequent Educational Priority Area (EPA) schemes did lead to many local initiatives, particularly in the inner city and immigrant areas, no national programme emerged, chiefly for fiscal reasons. Through the EPA policy, playgroups and home visiting schemes brought young pupils, parents and teachers together in *informal* educative environments and situations. A focus on specific and possibly prescriptive objectives, associated with the formalities of curriculum design, was avoided in favour of a more collaborative mode of working. However much this continuing community based work can lack specificity, it overcomes one of the dangers which Stern had recognised, namely that:

> *If* [author's italics] parenthood is largely a matter of attitudes and emotions, then intensive training in skills and the acquisition of knowledge are not only of little importance; they may be positively harmful, because parents, overwhelmed with advice and counsels of perfection, may become anxious and discouraged.

While the effective teaching principle of the need to support and encourage learners may here be granted, the fact that attitudes and emotions are at least partially conditioned by knowledge, understanding and skills also needs to be made. EFP objectives concerned with developing emotional dispositions must also incorporate cognitive and motor development if they are to be achieved.

The most recent official educational report which has explored the respective dimensions of parenthood preparation in schools and the wider possibilities of education for parents is *A Language for Life* (Bullock Report, 1975). This enquiry was concerned with reading and pupils' use of the English language. Of its many recommendations, a significant proportion lie essentially in the EFP field: for example, the increased involvement of secondary stage pupils in the care of young children, particularly in playgroups, both to assist in language development and to observe early learning in progress; and help for parents in the selection and use of books at home for early reading experiences. So far, however, the funds to implement most of Bullock's many proposals have not been forthcoming, although the report was widely applauded upon publication.

Throughout the post-war period there has been a great deal of advice and information available to parents through books, magazine articles, radio and television, but this has not reached many areas of need. In a direct sense, health visitors, maternity and child welfare centres/clinics, and some general practitioners have provided parent education, if only mainly for existing or expectant mothers. In 1961 the British Medical Association (BMA) suggested that it might undertake training courses for parents parallel to those begun in 1929 through the parent education movement in France; the BMA has now for many years produced a free book for newly-married couples on marriage and family life which has been widely read. Nevertheless, the patterns of action are sporadic, and it is a pity that many good isolated experiments have not been written-up and published.

The work of the National Marriage Guidance Council (NMGC) in marriage preparation by group discussion was recognised by Stern in 1960, and he noted that the groups were concerned with many aspects of family responsibilities, interpersonal attitudes and child development. From 1957, NMGC instituted specific training for educational groupwork for its volunteer counsellors who, upon invitation, have executed considerable work in schools, colleges and youth clubs in the sphere of 'Education and Personal Relationships', in addition to marriage preparation for engaged couples' groups. NMGC without doubt played an important catalytic role in the 1950s and 1960s through its conferences, training workshops and summer schools. Through those activities, teachers and youth leaders returned to their work to press their LEAs to develop parallel local in-service provision and to devise appropriate work schemes. However, like all non-statutory charitable bodies, NMGC has had limited funds, and from about 1967 when it integrated training for its educational and remedial work, and had begun to see the fruits of its initiatives within a good number of local authorities, priorities were somewhat restructured and NMGC's specifically educational work declined. There are now (late 1979) new plans to expand NMGC's educational initiatives which can build upon the earlier traditions and an educational projects officer has been appointed.

During the 1960s, as concern with adolescents' attitudes to sex and their social behaviour generally triggered off somewhat more positive and inclusive approaches to sex education and relationships, health education began to include preventive endeavours with respect to drug, alcohol and tobacco abuse. Interest also became concentrated upon the problems of non-accidental injury to young children, broken homes, and the apparent perpetuation of many personal and social disadvantages upon which traditional educational investments were not appearing to have much impact. Hence from around 1970 the term 'cycle of deprivation' gained professional currency, and during his four-year period in office as Secretary of State for Social Services, Sir Keith Joseph took this concept more explicitly into the political arena, though his initiatives were not incompatible with the earlier Educational Priority Areas policies. In 1972, at a conference of the Pre-school Playgroups Association, Sir Keith raised the question as to whether a cycle of deprivation underlay some of society's persistent social problems, and speculated whether a policy of preparation for parenthood could play a part in breaking it; preventive social policy in a fundamental sense was, he believed, a proper objective for the government. Encouraged by the warmth of public and professional response to such concepts he initiated in conjunction with the then Secretary for Education (Mrs Thatcher) a wide range of discussions with interested parties, the results of which were published as two important DHSS booklets in 1974 entitled *Preparation for Parenthood* and *Dimensions of Parenthood,* which commenced a new series of publications under the general title of 'The Family in Society'. Sir Keith also set up the official Court Committee to investigate the child care and health services; Court reported in 1976 and included positive references to parent and pre-parent education within the content of a wide preventive strategy.

* The greatest single need in medicine in the next 25 years is to give prevention the degree of scientific and educational attention that has been given in the last 25 years to treatment.

* Attention to improving an individual's general ability to cope with life . . . should be a primary objective of schools. To the extent that is achieved, it will help pupils to cope better in the future as parents.

* The programme within the school curriculum cannot be just a 'course' . . . it must be concerned with the whole development of the pupils' personality and concerned to promote knowledge of certain principles at appropriate stages. Nor can it be confined to the period . . . at school; opportunities must be found to improve understanding of these principles when the parents are actually meeting the problems . . . when there will be a reality to what they learn.

This period also saw the commissioning of scholarly literature reviews by DHSS which eventually led to Mia Kellmer Pringle's *The Needs of Children* and Michael Rutter and Nicola Madge's *Cycles of Disadvantage*. However, with the fall of the Conservative Government in 1974, and notwithstanding the Labour Party's traditional support for the family unit, there was a significant loss of political momentum over the next four years as reducing inflation became the national preoccupation, until family-based rhetoric appeared prominent in the run-up of both major parties to the 1979 General Election. The reorganisation of local government (1974) resulted in a number of temporary dislocations in services, and EFP initiatives, so often based upon volunteers and goodwill, also seem to have suffered through the many changes of administrative personnel which were involved. The DHSS hopes of action espoused in 1973 through the development of 'a programme of diverse activities' of EFP in liaison with the Department of Education and Science (DES) and other parties, and the promise 'to give further account of them', seem to have been overtaken by other priorities, and there have been no additions to their promising 'The Family in Society' series. The Preparation for Parenthood Group (see Appendix 1) in its small way has been able to keep the topic alive in the minds of civil servants, and in the longer term the 1978 White Paper on *Violence to Children,* which was issued by no fewer than seven central government departments, may prove to be a further significant milestone in establishing widespread preventive care for all parents and children, not simply those families at risk of non-accidental physical injuries.

The White Paper grew out of an all-party select committee enquiry, and a few examples of the committee's policy recommendations which were related to the field of EFP, using both formal and self-help strategies, were listed earlier (page 61). EFP was thus to be envisaged as a cooperative coordinated service provided not only by education authorities, but also through local authority social services departments, health authorities and voluntary agencies.

The committee's recommendations in this field were accepted by the government within a framework which stressed the importance of the family, caring relationships and the development of a sense of personal responsibility. The 1977 Green Paper *Education in Schools,* which succeeded the so-called 'Great Debate' on education, while giving the impression that the aim of preparing youngsters for the world of work was the top priority for curricular attention, also recommended that children of both sexes should learn how to cope with domestic tasks and with parenthood. Recently, a 1979 discussion paper from the Advisory Council for Adult and Continuing Education includes 'education for individual development and family life' as one of its five examples for development in that sphere, while a well researched report on pregnancy at school, produced by the National Council for One-Parent Families, incorporates several recommendations for EFP.

In summary, therefore, while we see that the field of EFP has been marked by numerous official approvals and many relatively isolated examples of practical innovation by enthusiasts (see below and Appendix 2), no UK government has developed any clear avenues of implementation in what is undoubtedly a complex field, academically, professionally and administratively. Concern is widespread, yet diffuse, while exhortation is one of the main features of the political discussions surrounding EFP. Perhaps somewhat unfortunately the legitimate equivocations of 'experts' drawn together for the 1973 DHSS Oxford discussion and recorded in *Dimensions of Parenthood,* which accentuate the complexities of research and what is unknown rather than what is known and shared, have given politicians a welcome excuse to let market forces operate. Meanwhile, the social and educational repair bills mount as we continue to vacillate about prevention. The fact that we do not know very much about the most effective techniques within an overall strategy of prevention should not delay us from committing ourselves experimentally to it. Part of the dilemma is reflected in this 1974 statement from the British Association of Social Workers:

> The parental role in this country today is not supported by a clear consensus of ideas about how parents should behave. While some may lament this situation, there is no choice but to recognise that it exists and to work from there.

A NOTE ON DEVELOPMENTS IN OTHER COUNTRIES

In Australia EFP appears to be in a relatively embryonic state, though the 1977 Royal Commission on Human Relationships was urged in many submissions to establish parent education programmes. In New Zealand intentions and action seem to be approximately equivalent to those in the UK, notwithstanding the relatively centralised educational system appropriate to its population level. In Canada, although there is significant academic influence from the USA and sporadic innovation, political and administrative initiatives do not seem to have brought about widespread developments.

On the European continent, France has a well-established 'School of Parents' in Paris with provincial centres. The 'School', while independent, is supported by the Ministries of Education and Health. It undertakes activities to stimulate public interest, executes training and acts as a focus for experiment and dissemination. Also in Paris is the headquarters of the International Federation for Parent Education founded in 1964 and working for the advancement of EFP and family living throughout the world. Having member groups from over 40 different countries, and links with UNESCO and UNICEF, it believes that EFP is an essential part of the lifelong learning process and should be included in local, state and national systems of continuing education in every country. In Luxembourg, which since 1951 has had a Department for Family and Population attached to the Ministry of Education, there is a comprehensive family policy in which educational programmes feature prominently. The topics of marriage, parenthood, school and family, with moral education, health, home-making and legal issues are a part of the school curriculum.

It is however in the USA where perhaps the highest investments in EFP have been made, some of the latest of which are outlined in Appendix 2 (pages 138–40). The Child Study Association of America was founded in 1888 by parents who wanted to make use of the knowledge and help of experts in the upbringing of their children, and the history of initiatives is a relatively long one. The US National Council of Parent Education was established in 1925, and in 1930 a White House Conference considered parent education as a way of confronting 'all the problems facing family life'. A further such meeting in 1960 recommended that family life courses including marriage and parent preparation be instituted as an integral and major part of public education, while 1980 has seen a similar event initiated by President Carter.

In his 1960 review Stern pointed to a vigorous and spontaneous parent education movement in the USA nourished by much research on child development and family relations; it was estimated that over 60% of schools provided courses on family living starting at the elementary grades and including psychological as well as practical aspects. The picture may not however have been as rosy as Stern's review suggested, for Somerville in 1971 recorded some major difficulties in implementing EFP programmes, which can no doubt be echoed elsewhere:

- (a) problems of specifying objectives and the low academic status accorded to EFP;
- (b) the lack of adequately prepared teachers and appropriately defined professional standards for family life and sex educators;
- (c) confusion of academic and administrative responsibility between school and college departments for EFP which requires input from several disciplines;
- (d) reluctance to modify existing timetables and traditional classroom procedures; and
- (e) low male participation among both students and teachers.

Nevertheless there is a wealth of published material in the USA for schools, colleges, youth groups and adults, which must at least reflect its commercial viability, and Benjamin Spock has been succeeded by new 'gurus', including Thomas Gordon, deviser of *Parent Effectiveness Training*.

The Carnegie Council on Children, set up by the Carnegie Corporation in 1972, has recently produced an important series of cross-disciplinary studies regarding the total welfare of children and families in America. The Council's concern arose in part from the dilemmas faced by policy-makers in combating social and educational disadvantage among children. Many initiatives took aspects of child development and pre-school experience in relative isolation from other contextual factors, such as parental involvement, employment, housing and the law. Early evaluation studies of the massive pre-school project 'Headstart', for example, had not been uniformly encouraging regarding the measurable longer term gains in school performance and adjustment of children, except where significant parental involvement had been achieved, hence the need to consider the total family context and not simply the educational programme.

Although the Council advocates a rational approach to child and family services within a comprehensive policy framework, EFP seems hardly to have been considered as a means for improving parental confidence and competence. The progressive usurping of the parental role by the various public services, while leaving parents with an ill-defined coordinating responsibility, may be noted, yet the restoration of parental dignity and authority is not simply an issue of political advocacy for more parental power through modifications to the socio-economic and sociolegal systems. It involves the development through education of relevant understanding, knowledge and skills, for power which is uninformed and which lacks the ingredients of competence is dangerous in any context. It seems that the Council may have too hastily written off earlier EFP initiatives as a means for changing the family lifestyles of large numbers of people, and it does not seem to have been able to consider the considerable developments arising from Federal Government grants during the mid 1970s (see page 138). Educational intervention may be a weak force on its own, but not necessarily if complemented by compatible social policies, and such issues are addressed in Chapter 6.

THE PRESENT SITUATION IN SCHOOLS

> *If by some strange chance not a vestige of us descended to the remote future save a pile of our school books or some college examination papers, we may imagine how puzzled an antiquary of the period would be on finding in them no sign that the learners would ever be parents. 'This must have been the curricula for their celibates,' we may fancy him concluding.*

Herbert Spencer (1870)

Over recent years many local education authorities and several examining boards have developed relatively broadly based courses for pupils and students of both sexes with varied titles such as 'Education for Personal Relationships', 'Education for Living', 'Child Care in the Family', 'Parentcraft' and so on. Some courses concentrate upon the tasks of setting up and maintaining a home, including the financial aspects, others are directed towards early child care, while others are concerned chiefly with the moral, personal and social development of the individual, including sex education. Some examples of current syllabuses are given in Appendix 2. However, much of what is available does not form a part of a core curriculum for everyone, and hence the administrative strategy for preparation for parenthood, like other fields which are crucial for later well-being, is fundamentally flawed.

With curriculum control essentially being based upon the individual school, and with the many other recent pressures upon and changes within the school system as a whole, including a range of other curriculum developments in established school subjects, it is difficult to gain accurate information regarding the provision of and access to experience by pupils in the preparation for parenthood field. Some student survey figures are however available.

As part of the National Child Development Study, the National Children's Bureau in 1974 followed up the sixteen-year-old population of about 12,000 youngsters born in one week of March 1958, with an approximately even division between boys and girls. This gave information about sex and parenthood lessons received at school which is abstracted in Tables 8 and 9 (below and page 78).

*Table 8*

*Boys and girls receiving no sex education instruction at school by age 16*

|  | % not receiving instruction | |
| --- | --- | --- |
| Topic | Boys | Girls |
| Reproduction | 12 | 7 |
| Emotional aspects | 35 | 28 |
| Contraception | 46 | 40 |
| Venereal disease | 36 | 30 |

Slightly more recent data from the Scottish Educational Data Archive relating to Scottish school leavers regarding their last year at school (the S4 stage for the academic year 1975–6) are shown in Tables 10 and 11 (pages 78, 79).

Most recently a secondary school survey executed in the spring of 1979 by the British Federation of University Women (BFUW) as a part of their contribution to the International Year of the Child, discovered that 24% of pupils from 151 schools in England and Wales take a course which includes child care and development. Within these courses as a whole, girls outnumbered boys by 4 to 1, and of these boys, only 1 in 5 studied on optional courses, tending to be discouraged from participation when male teachers are in charge of options, advice and

*Table 9*

*Sex and parenthood lessons at school by age 16*

|                                    | % of about 12,000 pupils who |                  |
| Topic                              | (a) received lessons | (b) wanted more |
| ---------------------------------- | :------------: | :------------: |
| How babies are conceived           | 76             | 13             |
| How babies are born                | 74             | 16             |
| How people get venereal disease    | 57             | 36             |
| The care of babies                 | 32             | 55             |
| How children grow and develop      | 51             | 38             |
| Practical problems of family life  | 40             | 57             |

Source: *Britain's Sixteen-Year-Olds* (National Children's Bureau, 1976)

*Table 10*

*Curriculum areas studied by Scottish school leavers 1975–6*

|   |                     | % following at S4 stage | | |
|   | Area of study       | Boys | Girls | All |
| - | ------------------- | :--: | :---: | :-: |
| 1 | Social education    | 19   | 23    | 21  |
| 2 | Health education    | 11   | 21    | 16  |
| 3 | Child care          | 1    | 11    | 6   |
|   | None of 1 to 3      | 73   | 58    | 65  |

administration. The survey suggested that the majority of courses are both aimed at and taken by pupils in the lower percentiles of the ability range, with 42% taking non-examined courses (V. Rubinstein, 1979).

These data, and those in the four Tables 8 to 11, indicate clearly that there is a long way to go before adequate provision is made with respect to preparation for parenthood. So long as education, in some of its concerns necessary for adequate human functioning in the modern

*Table 11*

*Demand for formal certification\* in certain curriculum areas by Scottish school leavers 1975–6*

|  | | % demand for certification by areas studied or not studied at S4 stage | | | |
|  | | Boys | | Girls | |
| Area of study | | Studied | Not studied | Studied | Not studied |
|---|---|---|---|---|---|
| 1 | Social education | 6 | 5 | 7 | 10 |
| 2 | Health education | 5 | 4 | 14 | 17 |
| 3 | Child care | 0 | 1 | 34 | 38 |
|  | All of 1 to 3 | 8 | | 43 | |

\* Scotland has a single system of public examinations at 'O' (Ordinary) and 'H' (Higher) grade and at the time of writing no equivalent to the Certificate of Secondary Education (CSE)

world, is left to the vagaries of the exercise of curricular options within each school, inadequate coverage will remain. However, there are indications of untapped reservoirs of positive pupil motivation, though until we can shift some of the traditional and now damaging adolescent and adult sex role perceptions, few boys seem to wish to have a public examination certificate marked with the subject 'Child care'! The effects of recent equal opportunities legislation, which includes reference to the school curriculum, should, in the long-term at least, redress some of the female bias. Such a hope however is not an adequate substitute for action in relation to the content of a life-relevant core curriculum constructed regardless of the sex of pupils.

Deficiencies in the school curriculum below the minimum leaving age of sixteen do not seem to be compensated for within the curricula of the comparatively few older adolescents who stay in some kind of full or part-time education. In the 1979 BFUW survey referred to above, only five of 119 courses appearing in the analysis were available for pupils aged sixteen to eighteen, 98% of participating pupils being aged fourteen to sixteen. Indeed, owing to the specialised character of the

British sixth form, topics of general interest or practical utility are
given low priority as the figures in Table 12 suggest.

*Table 12*

*Sixth form curriculum surveys on topics of general and practical interest*
A    *Percentages of 943 students who had in their sixth form years, 1973-5:*

| Subject | Competently dealt with | Touched on | None |
|---|---|---|---|
| Sex education | 10 | 27 | 62 |
| Family life | 13 | 13 | 73 |

| B          Year of survey | 1950 | 1975 |
|---|---|---|
| Sixth form sample size | 296 | 943 |

| Topic | % with no provision | |
|---|---|---|
| Sex education | 56 | 62 |
| How legal system works | 63 | 64 |
| Trade unionism | 52 | 52 |
| Politics | 42 | 46 |
| Economics | 62 | 62 |
| World history | 48 | 53 |
| Different religions | 43 | 48 |

C    *Percentage of 427 students receiving guidance (in 1973-5) on:*

| Health education | 22 | Taxation | 19 |
|---|---|---|---|
| Social security | 15 | Insurance | 18 |
| Careers | 65 | House purchase | 17 |

Of course, few of these topics assist directly with university or college
entrance, and there are no formal entry hurdles to parenthood. Of the
Scottish school leavers in 1976 who presented themselves for 'H' grade
(age 17+), only 14% had received social education during their last

school year; comparable figures for health education and child care were 11% and 1% respectively.

Perhaps the most reliable *serious* participation rates in relevant school courses are reflected by the numbers of entries to public examinations in subjects strongly related to preparation for parenthood. Whether we fully approve of it or not, the secondary school curriculum is predominantly examination oriented and in such a climate it is hard for non-examined topics to be treated really seriously by pupils, teachers and parents. Recent replies from the fourteen CSE and eight GCE (General Certificate of Education) Examining Boards received by the National Children's Bureau showed the overall picture indicated by Table 13.

*Table 13*

*Entries to public examinations in subjects related to child care and development 1978*

| *Examination/Type* | *Number of Boards* | | *Candidates* |
|---|---|---|---|
| | *Offering* | *Considering* | |
| CSE external (mode 1) | 7 | 1 | 13,188 |
| CSE internal (mode 3) | 9 | 1 | 3,831 |
| GCE 'O' level external* | – | – | – |
| GCE 'O' level internal | – | 3 | – |
| Certificate of Extended Education | 1 | – | 21 |
| GCE 'A' level* | – | – | – |

* 4 GCE Boards reported some related syllabus topics covered within the subjects Human Biology, Sociology, Psychology, Integrated Humanities, Domestic Science, Home Economics, Religious Studies and Home and Community Studies.

The courses to which the table refers are all relatively new, and growth in CSE entries has been rapid, from about 1000 in 1973 and 10,000 in 1976 to the present figures. If the 6732 school candidates taking the National Association for Maternal and Child Welfare courses (see Appendix 2, pages 147–9) in 1978 are added to the figures in Table 13, we see that, despite recent large increases in the availability of properly examined parent preparation courses, only about 3% of pupils in a national year's age group of about 700,000 are taking them;

comparable figures for biology and chemistry, for example, are approximately 50% and 25% respectively. A pilot survey by the BFUW, also for 1978, showed that within two CSE regions of relatively high activity in this field (Yorkshire and the West Midlands) only 11% of schools offered parentcraft and related courses, with but 2% of their total candidates taking them, of whom only one in 2000 was a boy.

Despite the fact that these figures present a probably over-pessimistic view due to the very real, if restricted, contributions being made through the quite popular subjects (with girls) of Home Economics and Human/Social Biology, there is still a very long way to go before parentcraft becomes both widespread and academically respectable in schools. Many of the existing courses in Home Economics and Health Education avoid explicit focus on EFP, and have a somewhat factual emphasis which can be more easily assessed by examinations. Yet adequate teaching in the EFP and child care fields needs to incorporate the emotional dimensions and the decisions which lie at the heart of all caring relationships. Though these are difficult to handle sensitively in the classroom context, to avoid them is to lead pupils into the naive and possibly dangerous assumption that adequate performance in this area is simply a matter of more factual learning.

An experienced teacher and social worker expressed her beliefs as follows:

'Education in personal relationships is more important at school than child development studies. Skills of child care can always be taught later, but relating to others becomes progressively more difficult to acquire later on. So many case histories involving child care problems seem to originate because the adults have inappropriate expectations of the opposite sex. All have insecurities about acceptance and trust, and cannot relate honestly and openly to others about things of crucial importance to them as persons . . . Of course there is a difference between teaching and experience, and formal education must go through a metamorphosis, particularly in terms of respectful trust between teachers and pupils, before book learning can really come alive.'

While there is plenty in the EFP field which can be made intellectually challenging for those students who can manage it, and upon this at least some of the future esteem of EFP must depend, a narrow academicism must be avoided; truly educational courses are academic *and* social *and* practical.

PREPARATION FOR PARENTHOOD: A PLACE IN THE SCHOOL
CURRICULUM FOR ALL PUPILS

A teacher in a secondary school for delicate and maladjusted children
with IQs ranging from 60+ to 140+ writes:

> 'Our course in 'Good Parenting' runs for one hour per week for both
> sexes in the final year. We initiated it in 1974 because of our concern
> about parental handling; poor handling seemed to lead to inade-
> quate parents in the next generation.'

The Headteacher of an inner city primary school writes:

> 'Although only a few of our children suffer from financial hard-
> ships, many have backgrounds which include acute social problems
> and parental neglect. The children about whom deepest concern is
> felt often seem to come from homes where little or no attention is
> given to their growth and development, and where there is usually
> no attempt to train or discipline . . . I came to the conclusion that
> part of the answer is to tackle the problem of inadequate parenting
> when it couldn't insult or offend—before people usually became
> parents while they are still at secondary school . . . Surely the
> inclusion on the timetable of these subjects *for everyone* would
> establish in future parents' minds that bringing up children is a task
> important enough not to be left to chance, to be given some of the
> precious short school day.'

Because of the British tradition that the school curriculum is a matter
for the schools themselves, Religious Education is the only compulsory
subject laid down by the 1944 Education Act. Consequently the
curriculum has become the site for competing bids from different
groups at the local authority and, especially, school level. Hence the
curriculum as a whole when viewed at any level above the individual
school, and often even within the school, is disaggregated, idiosyn-
cratic and incoherent. With the reorganisation of secondary education
on comprehensive lines over the past 25 years, and the consequent
creation of larger school units, for pupils from the age of thirteen or
fourteen onwards the curriculum has been characterised by an array of
options, devised by individual schools. These have favoured pupils'
individual choice at the expense of shared experiences in socially
desirable fields. This policy creates annually for schools large administrative problems, and, at least until relatively recently, has
deflected attention away from adequate consideration and implementation of what comprehensive education might mean in terms of the
content and activities of the curriculum.

Here it is inappropriate to go into the detailed analysis and justification of the characteristics of a balanced general education for all (see, for example, Whitfield 1971, 1978). There is however a developing consensus that at least until the age of sixteen all school pupils should maintain studies in subjects and topics which will continue to develop understanding and skills in seven areas:

1  mathematical understanding;
2  linguistic communication (particularly English);
3  scientific studies (physics, chemistry, biology, rural science, etc);
4  aesthetic activities (art, crafts, music, etc);
5  personal and social development;
6  historical, environmental and religious perspectives;
7  physical activities.

These areas have received the approval of HM Schools Inspectorate.

It seems likely that this kind of list will feature strongly in any later debates about a core curriculum and its monitoring, but pressures to emphasise the learning of basic skills and topics to ensure national economic and industrial well-being tend to relegate the more personal and socially-oriented subjects to a lesser role. The somewhat greater problems of professional agreement about aims and of evaluating 'results' of social education programmes, compared with those in, say, mathematics and science, is a further disincentive to taking them very seriously as curricular time is distributed by senior school staffs and their advisers. But we must recognise that divergencies of curricular priorities to some extent reflect different conceptions of the social order and are thus fundamentally moral in character.

Clearly 'preparation for parenthood' lies chiefly, though not exclusively, within the 'personal and social development' area, in which understanding the self and other persons is a crucial aim. Since the possibility of parenthood, or at least child care, is real for all, and has such pervasive consequences, there are excellent grounds for making proper consideration of it compulsory for all pupils during some period of their secondary education. The many utilitarian arguments for such a policy are not in the least incompatible with academic arguments about education and the development of mind in particular modes of human consciousness. Within schools there is a captive audience, at least apart from truants, and the evidence on the largely favourable attitudes of pupils should be taken seriously, for other areas are not necessarily more highly valued by pupils as a whole. With few exceptions, from the onset of puberty, adolescents have a fascination with procreative and reproductive processes, so that motivation in this area is strong and can with advantage be turned to raising issues relating to the care and nurture of children and the responsibilities of parenthood.

It should be made clear that a single national course is not in any way being suggested. Even if appropriate evaluation had taken place, the diversity of pupils, and of teaching contexts and teachers, necessitates some genuine diversity within a framework of agreed principles and topic areas. The general aim is to help youngsters to grow into parenthood through the exercise of informed choices. Finding a place in the core curriculum for EFP activities is the key issue, and in the author's view, this should not be delayed by discussion regarding the desirability or otherwise of formal examination, upon which there is a conflict of interests: for example, 'failing' in 'parent-craft' can hardly be a justified outcome for a group of pupils. The BFUW survey (page 77) found that 10% of their responding schools had adopted a two-tier approach with all their pupils taking a non-examined compulsory course in, for example, Social Education, with the choice of further optional examined courses. In fact, one third of pupils in that survey, representing only 9% of the secondary school population, were taking compulsory non-examined courses in child development.

The BFUW survey concluded that: 'this subject is of such fundamental importance to future family welfare that non-examined courses should be available to every secondary school pupil, and should be compulsory' (V. Rubinstein, 1979). The Secretary of State for Education's discussion document, *A Framework for the School Curriculum* (DES, January 1980) is encouraging to this end.

## STAFFING AND ORGANISATION

It is relatively easy to advocate national parent preparation and education programmes; it is far less simple to implement them without a massive training programme of suitable teachers from schools and further education. Curriculum implementation depends upon teachers, and a large increase in the number of male teachers qualified to do the required teaching will be necessary if more boys are to be attracted to the courses, unless they are made compulsory. For example, although Home Economics is now an optional subject open to boys as well as girls, the Inner London Education Authority has only one male Home Economics teacher.

The teacher-qualities which would seem essential are not necessarily much different from those which research suggests promote successful learning in other fields, that is warmth of manner, the kinds of demands made, flexibility of approach and conceptual clarity. In addition to these one might add the ability to be both open and genuine with students and not embarrassed by any of the topics which they may raise. These qualities are not necessarily age-dependent, but clearly those who have raised or who are raising their own families, or who have alternative contact with young children and have experienced stress and problems first-hand, will be at some advantage over those whose knowledge may have been less directly experienced. And in a sensitive field of this kind volunteers, who are prepared to take further training as necessary, rather than coerced substitutes, are essential. The nature of the work requires that the teachers concerned must have come to terms with their own personal lives. Those who have not resolved their own inner conflicts about relationships could find that studying child development and family life brings these to the surface, leading to a strained classroom atmosphere which could be unsettling for the students. Teachers thus further qualified as school or college counsellors may have a key role to play in the coordination of the relevant aspects of the curriculum.

While at present there may be insufficient personnel of a suitable kind formally qualified in teaching for the tasks ahead (and this is especially true of men), a wide range of others can and do make valuable contributions—not simply local social workers and health authority personnel, but also marriage guidance counsellors, community service volunteers and individuals associated with organisations such as the Samaritans. The contribution which ordinary parents could also make under guidance should not be underestimated, but this requires flexible and respectful attitudes towards the use of such help. There could be the additional advantage that the participation of several adults from different walks of life might help to avoid the implication of a single style of family life and of highly prescriptive parental skills.

Like much else in the school curriculum, courses having parent preparation objectives, if they are to be successful, require the enthusiastic support of the headteacher. Most of these courses that are at present in operation take place, as we have noted, between the ages of thirteen and sixteen. The timetabling of them is crucial if practical experience with young children and other external visits are to be possible. A half-day block is ideal, since two split single periods of about 40 minutes do not allow the flexibility required for the essential practical experience. The difficulty lies in the nature of the school options system. Timetabling arrangements that suit one option do not always suit another to which it is parallel. This difficulty must be overcome, but in the meantime much valuable related work can be done through more conventional subjects that *can* be fitted into the existing timetabling patterns, although for them to be really effective, even this may entail some administrative difficulty.

Because the boundaries of EFP are not as clearly discernible as for some subjects, and several staff are likely to be involved in the meeting of EFP objectives, an informed coordinator is likely to be necessary in most schools to dovetail syllabus elements, to avoid unnecessary overlap, and to liaise with and encourage staff, including external helpers. Poorly organised and unconnected course units could do more harm than good, and effectively innoculate students against later essential instruction. The relatively circumscribed two-year examination courses in 'Child Development and the Family', while undoubtedly being attractive administratively, are unlikely in the short term to be feasible for all pupils, and a number of core experiences may, with administrative skill, be provided in other ways. A policy for native language development across the curriculum has been widely discussed in the 1970s and ratified by the Bullock Report. Something similar seems necessary in the fields of social, health and moral education despite the very real difficulties of administration and monitoring in an examination oriented and subject based curriculum. A key task of the coordinator would be to ensure that all pupils, regardless of their subject options, received those experiences upon which their later well-being in these fields could depend.

One of the Aston-based research projects (see Appendix 3) will be exploring both administrative and teaching practice, including the extent to which agreement can be obtained among the various interest groups regarding core topics for syllabuses. However, the possibility of only limited consensus must at this stage be recognised. Whatever the arrangements, school and college level courses should not arouse fear and anxiety in young people about their possible future roles. Implied criticism of their own home circumstances should also be avoided, since most parents try to do their best for their children, and failure is often the result of ignorance or unavoidable stress.

In linking with pre-school organisations for practical experience there is a need to find playgroups and nursery classes which have an atmosphere somewhere between simple unpurposeful childminding and rigidly structured activities in which there is no freedom of expression and learning through play. Adolescents need to see how young children develop when given a rich and stimulating environment with free communication and an unobtrusive organisation. Should school courses further increase in popularity there could well become a shortage of pre-school groups suitable for observation and participation, and this will necessitate careful coordination. Already some Inner London schools are experiencing difficulties in this respect. *If* however primary school accommodation and equipment which becomes redundant as a result of the fall in the birth rate is used for expanding pre-school and daycare activities, then this problem might be solved. But first, preparation for parenthood must gain a far more pervasive foothold in the curriculum, as a core component, in the author's view. Intervention at the time of marriage and the first baby is not soon enough. However, to reach this desirable objective will require external political initiatives to augment the existing experimentation and goodwill in the schools; presently, as we have noted, there is some prospect of this.

PROVISION BEYOND SCHOOL

One advantage of taking preparation for parenthood seriously at school level is that there alone exists a relatively captive audience. Beyond school it is commonplace for those most needing guidance to be the most difficult to draw into the net of provision. What seems essential is a wide range of sources and styles of help to satisfy differing adult needs and motivations. If appropriate foundations, especially in the realm of attitudes, have been laid at school there will be a greater prospect of a responsible seeking out of advice, support and encouragement later, when the need for knowledge and skills is actual or imminent. In EFP in particular the possibility of making secondary schools open for adult students is worthy of serious consideration. Besides the mutual enrichment of teenager and mature student, such an arrangement would make prudent use of precious resources. It will be recalled that the need for greater school openness was mentioned in Chapter 2 (page 16).

If one excludes those training for the child care professions, provision for EFP in further and higher education is difficult to assess, since the main thrust of the various courses is avowedly specialist and generally aimed at young unmarried adults beginning their careers. While many institutions, including a handful of universities such as Keele and Aston, have elements of general or complementary studies within their curricula for all students, it is no small challenge to teaching staff to maintain serious study and motivation in these programmes when the majority, if not all of the 'rewards' (that is, the degrees, diplomas and certificates) are vested within the specialised curriculum. We have noted that much the same situation pertains for the majority in school sixth forms, where A-level grades are the things that count in the career market place, rather than breadth of outlook acquired through a general studies programme.

However, such information as is available suggests that preparation for parenthood rarely forms a significant part of general studies courses, and in what little is done, more attention is given to the curative aspects of immediate student problems through health and counselling services than their prevention in both the short and long-terms. If suitably qualified and enthusiastic staff were available, there is reason to believe that many of these older students would find EFP topics within their general studies courses more attractive than many of the topics traditionally included in them. A small scale trial survey in 1979 of a random sample of 161 first year Aston undergraduates (mean age 19, 93% males) gave the results shown in Table 14.

*Table 14*

| Statement | % agreeing |
|---|---|
| There is no viable alternative to the nuclear family for most people | 70 |
| I come from a happy family | 85 |
| The job of being a parent is not very difficult | 7 |
| To be a parent needs training like any other skilled job | 53 |
| I need educational help before becoming a parent | 41 |
| I have no wish to become a parent | 8 |
| I think I would be a good parent | 77 |

Thus while there is a degree of confidence about their own likely performance as parents, these students tend to see the task as difficult, and a significant proportion of even this mainly male sample would welcome some formal preparation for parenthood. Under present provision it is doubtful whether they will receive it or even discover appropriate external agencies to meet their needs. The sample is very pro-family, scoring a mean of 85% on a 9-item 'family feelings' scale (reliability 0.6), and it would certainly be of interest to use this scale with other groups. It could well be that these able young people, the relative successes of the school system, have reached their present educational level at least partly because they have had largely happy home lives.

Once again the point has to be made that in our examination-oriented educational system, status tends to be accorded only to those subjects which are formally assessed, and EFP advocates must take note of this even though formal assessment is in some ways alien to some EFP objectives. There may be a case for developing some kind of national certificate in EFP for students beyond school, which could draw together the wide variety of *ad hoc* validating bodies with interests in the field such as the Royal Society of Health, the National Council for Home Economics and the National Association for Maternal and Child Welfare (see page 147). Such a certificate might be offered within a wide variety of institutions, helping to focus and strengthen parts of general studies, through a new body perhaps called the 'Parent Education Council'. This could in some ways be parallel to the Technician and Business Education Councils, yet able to draw in representatives from all interested institutions including universities, polytechnics and other Council for National Academic Awards (CNAA) validated colleges and institutes. Some common thread within higher and further education with an emphasis on human welfare could help to reduce divisiveness at that stage and build upon student idealism.

A range of important yet uncoordinated work goes on in the youth services, in local authority, church-based or other clubs for young people. Provision of EFP work in these is however patchy, and there seems to be more concentration of limited resources upon counselling and advisory services for those youngsters who have already revealed their personal difficulties. Whilst young people are particularly open to learning and change during a personal crisis, an increased emphasis upon preventive experience for all would seem desirable. Some developments using non-statutory youth service outlets have however taken place in the USA recently (see Appendix 2, page 139).

Naturally for any couple EFP becomes really pressing when they learn that they are expecting their first baby. For the woman at least all the medical assistance she is likely to require is freely available. Early confirmation of any pregnancy and ante-natal clinic attendance are important in reducing the risk of perinatal mortality and handicap (see also page 49). Yet something over 25% of mothers, particularly those who are young, unsupported, economically impoverished, or who already have large families, delay medical contact until well beyond the third or fourth month of pregnancy. This must at least in part stem from the fact that there is no obligation to prepare for parenthood. Most Area Health Authorities provide classes about preparation for the event of birth and in babycare, but provision seems fragmented and attendance less than satisfactory. Furthermore the midwives and health visitors giving the instruction appear to be very much left on their own in terms of the topics to cover and the length and style of presentation. Most midwifery services offer between five and ten classes, but at present only about one half of midwives have had any basic training for such teaching. The integration of men into the provision is clearly no small challenge, but clearly desirable if a relaxed atmosphere for learning is to be achieved. Since teaching time, given the resources presently available, is limited, inevitably most attention has to be directed to mothers having their first babies, and covering the stages of labour and the development of breathing skills. This means that help at this stage with more general issues of relationships, of coping emotionally and physically after the baby's birth, and with sibling rivalry (in the case of second and subsequent children) is therefore inevitably limited. The experience of adoptive parents is possibly even more one of 'immersion at the deep end'. Gillian Pugh's recent summary of the ante-natal class research certainly leaves no room for complacency.

The National Childbirth Trust (NCT) has had a notable influence on the attitudes of the medical profession towards making the act of birth enjoyable, with, when possible, fathers participating. In 1978 almost 10,000 women attended NCT fee-paying pre-natal classes, reflecting gaps in the statutory services, whether in terms of publicity, organisation, convenience or perceived value. The young mother is in many ways not short of advice from a wealth of books, magazines and pamphlets; television and 'phone-in radio in particular seem to be increasingly used as sources of information and help (see Appendix 2, pages 149–53). Whether mothers, and perhaps a few fathers, are able to discriminate between the conflicting information available from the 'experts' is however an open question, and the relationship between these less formal sources of help and ante-natal classes has scarcely been examined.

It is possible that the notion of formal classes for the necessary development of birth and early babycare skills can distract health service workers from attention to the more far-reaching changes in the relationships between parents, in lifestyles and economic circumstances, which the arrival of baby inevitably brings. Once we have understood the processes of transition to parenthood, it may well be that EFP activities at this crucial stage will pay more attention to the mutually supportive roles of mother and father. Research has shown that the birth of baby can reduce marital satisfaction, for there is a highly dependent new being demanding attention, often at unsocial hours. This new being does not appreciate that its long-term interests are bound up with the strength and richness of the marriage relationship, and with the personal well-being of mum and dad. At least some of the feelings of isolation and post-natal depression experienced by some mothers can be attributed to marital tensions, as baby, perhaps, somewhat unexpectedly for both mother and father, seems to them to drive a wedge between them.

After birth it is important that parents do not feel socially isolated, yet it is clear that many do, especially if they lack an informal network of friends, relatives and neighbours who understand their problems and their new and relatively cramped lifestyle. Most families have access to child health clinics, though, as at the pre-natal period, attendance by mothers is uneven and attention is directed much more at baby's needs than parental anxieties. Nevertheless there seems to be growth in the number and range of parent support schemes organised by both statutory and voluntary agencies which reduce isolation and aim to foster parental self-confidence. Health visitors and NCT branches are doing important work in setting up and maintaining small groups for mothers and their young children, to supplement more traditional home visiting schemes. Even in socially disadvantaged areas there is some evidence to suggest that neighbourhood support schemes, which draw on the abilities of families to help themselves, can enable parents with economic, housing and other personal problems to modify their lifestyles so that they take into account more fully some of the principles of child care. The concept of the family community centre is no longer new, and the rapid recent growth in mother and toddler and babysitting groups are further responses to the problems encountered by many of today's families. Parents are trying to find new ways of incorporating other known and trusted adults in the care of their children, and to reduce their own isolation, and some new and effective substitutes for the traditional extended family are emerging. Again, however, provision is patchy, the 'curriculum' unclear, and fathers are relatively rarely involved. A fund of goodwill and concern nevertheless exists with many giving their time voluntarily in home visiting and in playgroups for the sake of children.

Other voluntary but more specialised developments include 'Parents Helpline' and 'Parents Anonymous', both of which exist to help parents who have violent feelings towards their children. Parents Helpline facilitates problem-sharing parents groups, sometimes with the aid of a sympathetic professional; Parents Anonymous mainly uses a round-the-clock telephone service. In parallel with Alcoholics Anonymous, both schemes use first-names only, and the threat of punitive authority or of disabling disapproval is removed. The aim is to reach at least a part of the large pool of parents who feel and act violently towards their children while knowing that it is wrong for them to do so.

In more formal adult education, radio and television-initiated action seems full of promise. Recent initiatives by the TV and radio companies and the Open University (see pages 149–53) could have significant long-term impacts. Producers and administrators are experimenting with ways in which to encourage the TV viewer to be less passive in the reception of programme material. 'To view and then to do', be it to buy a support publication, write a letter, make a 'phone call, see a counsellor, or join a local group, may be an apt motto for the future.

Parent education may thus be a growing feature of our social life, but it is not yet seen as a necessary part of a community-based adult education service in which parents can formulate their values and practices reflectively, through group participation with other parents, and in relation to their own circumstances. A British Association for Family Education failed to get off the ground in 1973, but there are now several signs that a more coordinated national forum may be viable. Meanwhile existing services for families are giving at least some parents increased confidence, understanding and skills for the benefit of their children, who will make up a section of the next generation of parents.

## PROGRAMME EVALUATION

One of the disappointing features of EFP worldwide, and certainly in the UK, is the lack of monitoring and evaluation. Many apparently good ideas have not been properly tested and we have little knowledge of how best to proceed save from the anecdotal experiences of those enthusiasts who have been involved. All areas of educational evaluation present their problems, and within EFP they are likely to be severe since much of what those who are involved seek to achieve represents a long-term investment. The tasks for evaluation are not simply confined to problems of measuring knowledge and skills gained perhaps at the age of fifteen or sixteen or in ante-natal classes, for that in principle is possible, but also how effectively these are put to use, sometimes under stressful conditions, at varying lengths of time afterwards, when family problems are actually confronted.

Positive social effects from more widespread preventive action must certainly not be expected too soon, and many would argue that the fundamental aims of preparation for parenthood are concerned with developing positive attitudes and knowledge of sources of help when the time for parenthood arrives. While it seems likely that there may be a very limited retention of factual material after a few years, that hypothesis has not been tested, and insofar as pre-parent courses bring 'real life' into the school, which is so often perceived as detached from it, then the 'relevance' factor may make the learning even at that stage less transient. School courses leading to external examinations might just be reaching the stage and scale for some of the results to be provisionally assessed, and this aspect will be included in the Aston based secondary curriculum evaluation study recently commenced (see Appendix 3, pages 154–5).

The evaluation of EFP activities beyond and outside school has the advantage of being closer to the actual performance of parental skills, but the disadvantage of having to deal with a far more complicated pattern of sources of knowledge and experience. We know little about the advice and information sources used by parents, particularly after the infant stage, to help them in their parental roles, and this needs to be better charted before any more controlled comparative evaluation of parent education is possible. A further area of ignorance is in regard to the proportion of the total time spent on various activities by different types of family. Changes in patterns of time spent as a result of educational intervention would be one useful evaluative index since, perhaps not surprisingly, research at the school level has shown that the time divisions within the curriculum are related to the quantity and character of learning. It might, for example, be hypothesised that knowledge by parents relating to child development might lead to significant shifts in lifestyle from, say, less time spent passively ignoring young children to interacting with them in language and play activities. Another index might be based upon how the family income is spent, whether, for example, more is given to books and constructive toys than sweets.

At whatever level evaluation of EFP activities may in future be practised, it is important that the needs and wishes of the clients (adolescents and adults) are taken properly into account. The views of various professional experts, who can only usually argue from their specialised knowledge and limited field experience, must take into account the desires of those whom they seek to help. Whatever may be our community needs in this sphere, they must necessarily be diverse in both their character and presentation if they are to be grafted on to, and utilised within, the wide variety of social contexts and chosen lifestyles which exist in our democratic and pluralist society. That being the case, no simplistic standardised evaluation packages will meet our needs. However, the following areas will need to be considered within the spectrum of evaluation activities:

(a) assessment of needs and desires for information and services;

(b) measurement of knowledge of facts relevant to child care;

(c) estimation of attitudes towards child-rearing and of dispositions to take on the responsibilities of parenthood;

(d) measurement of the use made of the services provided and of the skills acquired by parents and parents-to-be; and

(e) longitudinal monitoring of effects of educational intervention upon child health, welfare and educational performance.

These represent a somewhat daunting task, but to intervene without a concomitant commitment to evaluate is to act blindly and, as curriculum developers have found at school level over the past fifteen years, widespread 'tissue rejection' could result with little practical guidance as to where to start afresh. It is, however, to be hoped that we are moving into a phase in which programme evaluation in the health, education and social services is regarded as an intrinsic part of development rather than an optional extra for the research minded. Provided evaluators are prepared to be eclectic regarding their methods of analysis and data collection techniques, moulding their activities around and within the action, rather than prescribing and restricting it through devotion to an input/output model which undervalues the processes of intervention, then there is a good chance that their work will be valued equally by practitioner and policy-maker. The literature on evaluation techniques and their rationales has grown tremendously in recent years, and though much of it has its origin in the USA, adaptation and extrapolation to other contexts and countries is now necessary if we are to take seriously the ethical requirement for social accounting of finite resources.

## PRIORITIES, AND SOME OBJECTIONS ANTICIPATED

All preventive educational initiatives need to be set within a wider framework of social policies for families, and this is the subject of the next chapter. When examining human dysfunctions within a micro arena, such as the family, there can easily be a temptation to regard problems as arising solely from the educational and psychological shortcomings of individuals. We now know that much human behaviour at the micro levels within our social structure is determined by economic and political forces shaped at the national and regional levels. We have only slowly and painfully discovered that social and educational interventions directed at relatively localised levels of the social structure have limited long-term pay-off. Education for parenthood must not therefore be seen as a relatively cheap and circumscribed means of avoiding some of the other central socio-economic factors which militate against effective child care and parental well-being.

Nevertheless, it is possible here to indicate some priorities for EFP development, and that means, at least initially, the catalytic involvement of professionals, building from promising examples of existing practice. Whilst it may be argued that the capacities of individuals, families and communities for self-help have been progressively undermined by the forward thrust of professional groups, there can be no turning back of the clock overnight to meet the majority of needs (see also Chapter 6, pages 116–19).

At school level the major priorities would seem to be to increase appropriate in-service training for teachers, and to develop social climates and administrative procedures in order to increase the attentive enrolment of boys in relevant course units. There is some evidence which suggests that in-service training is not expanding anything like enough to match the rate of course growth. A relatively small number of teachers are therefore carrying too many of the burdens of school-based development without the opportunity for reflective professional and personal growth, and the parallel related enrichment of those of their colleagues interested in becoming involved in a team approach to preparation for parenthood. The personal qualities needed by teachers for this sensitive field previously referred to (page 86) require unhurried development and consolidation if the staff are to feel secure and adequately prepared for their tasks. Training in group dynamics, role play and simulation techniques rarely formed a part of the initial training of the teachers now willing to take some of the responsibility for EFP. The adequate mediation of preparation for parenthood activities for boys is dependent upon staff development and greater male involvement, though relatively cosmetic factors such as changing a course title from, say, 'Child development' to Human development' might combat some of the existing unjustified social conditioning.

In further and higher education the viability of suitable courses in EFP will depend chiefly upon the availability of appropriately skilled staff for teaching general studies and related subjects. Personnel in the student health and chaplaincy services also have potential roles in this field. However, 'general studies' has usually been seen as explicitly non-vocational, and since parenthood is at its core a practical vocation, there may not be many existing staff who would feel a deep enough commitment to EFP for it to oust parts of present offerings in such courses. It is at the further and higher education level, however, that professional training for all those who are later to be involved in the care and education of children is given. Although some reforms are in progress to make such training more practical and relevant, there is a case for developing a common core to the training of residential workers, social workers, some medical personnel and teachers based upon child development yet fitted into the context of home and the opportunities existing there for the nurture of children's abilities. This shared experience by a range of fledgling professionals could not only encourage them to develop real partnerships with parents, but could also serve to acquaint them with the nature of the training and skills of each other's profession. The child care professions are often insulated not simply through institutional administration, but by mutual ignorance.

In adult education men need more encouragement to attend ante- and post-natal classes arranged at times suited to their other commitments, while a good social case could be argued for the use of television for EFP work at more convenient viewing times—a change which need not cost any money. Voluntary organisations likewise, for relatively little cost, could develop outreaches related to EFP and family support: the churches, for example, do not have a good record in terms of total family care, often tending to divorce the care of souls and the practice of worship from the wider social context of our time. Those who are willing to teach within EFP at any level would find a systematised bank of resource materials helpful, and consideration could be given to establishing a national resource centre. Certainly any further more formal curriculum development should await the collation of existing materials produced by publishers, teachers' centres and health-related bodies.

But EFP priorities will not be met without an unsilenceable chorus of commitment from a sufficient number of people who, upon reflection about the social and moral condition of our times, care enough about the well-being of children and those who look after them. That chorus of concern is growing, and it has three prime tasks. Firstly, it must attack the academic conservatism of the educational system, in which a disdain for the practical remains deeply engrained. 'Wise man', *homo sapiens,* encompasses 'making man', *homo faber,* and wisdom is knowledge *put to use* to feed and sustain man's identity. Home-making is thus a crucial objective for any nation, without which the value of other goals, such as liberal academic learning and industrial manufacture, is diminished. The second task is to demystify some of the professionalism surrounding the family and childrearing, while the third is to speak up for families and children whenever political, economic and social pressures seem likely to undermine their well-being.

But these tasks need courage, for there is opposition, not simply from those professionals with blinkered and protective vision about their skills, but probably more seriously from some liberal intellectuals who, in defence of democracy as they see it, would brook no 'interference' in the styles and lives of today's families, nor wish to modify the range of 'natural' behaviour in families-to-be. EFP, let us have no illusions, is every bit as delicate a topic as religious or political education within the ambience of a liberal democratic and pluralist society.

This author certainly recognises that ranged against his advocacy of including aspects of EFP in a core curriculum at school level there will be those who genuinely fear the possible early imposition of cultural lifestyles and forms of living on young people—such as the valuing of marriage above other forms of cohabitation, the perpetuation of inequalities between the sexes, the transmission of 'middle class' practice and so on. But as authors in the religious and political education fields have pleaded, a crucial distinction must be made between 'teaching about' and 'coercive conditioning or indoctrinating in' such subjects which lie close to matters of individual practice. Here concern has been with education *about* parenthood, not education *in* parenthood of a particular kind or style. In the end pupils and adults have to make up their own minds regarding personal action; the plea has simply been that they should do so on the basis of knowledge, rather than hearsay or ignorance, and against a background of love and concern for children.

But let it be noted that some of that knowledge is not devoid of implications for the *morality* of human action, an issue in which a community as a whole, if it is concerned about the rights of *all* its members, must have some over-arching concern through its socio-political and legal processes. The care and well-being of children by their parents or other adults is not solely a private matter. The State in the end has to be the guardian of the interests of those who have no political franchise, and must through its various arms of influence ensure that knowledge relevant to human welfare is disseminated. The State now does it in such fields as lead pollution, tobacco smoking, road safety, contraception and personal hygiene. In a nutshell, we need coordinated efforts to do likewise in the whole field of child care and parental support. No case is being made for the distillation of 'best practice' in parenthood, for that must vary according to circumstance, time and place, even within the most coherent of family lifestyles. The core of concern is for understanding by adolescents and adults of the potential effects of their actions, and inactions, upon the growth and maturation of babies and children, and an appreciation by them of the need for long-term commitment by some 'special adults' for the new-born child. Every child has the right to continuing, dependable loving care; to grow into a physically fit adult; to acquire emotional stability in order to remain resilient under the inevitable strains and stresses of life; and to develop its educational and intellectual potential for personal fulfilment and responsible citizenship.

A summary of precepts embodying the substance of the argument so far may seem obvious. The Newsons simply describe good parenting as 'warmth and willingness to take trouble'. With a little more sophistication here one can suggest the following:

Give the children in your care good food and adequate clothing; give them unbegrudgingly of your time, your consistent love, and increasing responsibility as they grow up. Create a rich and varied yet stable environment for them. Adapt your lifestyle partly, though not exclusively, to their needs for play, for friends and for reading and oral language experience. Remember each child is unique and, if you have more than one, 'standard' treatments are often not appropriate or effective. Praise pays and when giving rebuke make sure that your child understands that it is his behaviour you reject and not him as a person.

Yet these precepts of a balanced child-centredness cannot be understood, let alone consistently practised, without teaching and copious illustration with suitable examples prior to or during parenthood. So those concerned must sustain *the courage to teach* and reach out to learners in a values-sensitive area, and in a manner which is genuinely respectful of their backgrounds and aspirations.

Insofar as EFP has been defined as a specific part of moral and social education, implicitly these fields have been assumed to be the legitimate business of the education service and categorised, no less than scientific or aesthetic awareness, as 'pearls of great price' requiring some form of intergenerational succession. If it be argued that in practice the responsibilities of family members to each other grow to a great extent out of the feelings which they have for each other, then EFP is concerned with creating environments in which enrichment of these feelings becomes possible, rather than the alternatives of indifference, neglect, alienation and hostility which eat away our capacity for self-respect and damage others. While there may be many facets of EFP which are problematic, there are many others which are not, and a part of EFP must necessarily be concerned with aiding discrimination between these as a basis for responsible decision-making for child care, on both a communal and an individual basis. We do the community no educational service by avoiding even the most controversial issues, for it is in these that the 'curriculum' at any stage can reach close to life in its complexity, rather than remain a somewhat sterile, antiseptic shadow of reality.

## References

CENTRAL ADVISORY COUNCIL FOR EDUCATION (England) (1959). *15 to 18*. (The Crowther Report). London: HMSO.

CENTRAL ADVISORY COUNCIL FOR EDUCATION (England) (1963). *Half our Future*. (The Newsom Report). London: HMSO.

DALLAS, D. M. (1972). *Sex Education in School and Society*. Slough: NFER Publishing.

DEPARTMENT OF EDUCATION AND SCIENCE (1975). *A Language for Life*. (The Bullock Report). London: HMSO.

DEPARTMENT OF EDUCATION AND SCIENCE (1977). *Education in Schools: A Consultative Document*. London: HMSO.

DEPARTMENT OF EDUCATION AND SCIENCE (1977). *Curriculum 11-16*. (HMI report, December 1977). London: Department of Education and Science.

DEPARTMENT OF EDUCATION AND SCIENCE (1977). *Health Education in Schools*. London: HMSO.

DEPARTMENT OF HEALTH AND SOCIAL SECURITY (1974). *Preparation for Parenthood*. London: HMSO.

DEPARTMENT OF HEALTH AND SOCIAL SECURITY (1974). *Dimensions for Parenthood*. London: HMSO.

GORDON, T. (1970). *Parent Effectiveness Training*. New York: Wyden Books.

HERON, A. (1952). 'Adolescents and Preparation for Parenthood' in *British Journal of Educational Psychology*, 22 (3), pp. 173-9.

MINISTRY OF EDUCATION (1949). *Citizens Growing Up*. London: HMSO.

NATIONAL COUNCIL FOR ONE-PARENT FAMILIES (1979). *Pregnant at School*. London: National Council for One-Parent Families.

OGDEN, G., and ZEVIN, A. (1976). *When a Family Needs Therapy*. Boston, Mass.: Beacon Press.

PICKARTS, E., and FARGO, J. (1971). *Parent Education*. Englewood Cliffs, New Jersey: Prentice Hall.

PUGH, G. (ed.) (1980). *Preparation for Parenthood: Some Current Initiatives and Thinking*. London: National Children's Bureau.

REYNOLDS, C. (1975). *Teaching Child Development*. London: Batsford.

SCOTTISH EDUCATION DEPARTMENT (1979). *Health Education in Primary, Secondary and Special Schools in Scotland*. London: HMSO.

SOMERVILLE, R. M. (1971). 'Family Life and Sex Education in the Turbulent Sixties' in *Journal of Marriage and Family*, 33, pp. 11-35.

STERN, H. H. (1956). 'Parent Education and Parental Learning'—unpublished PhD thesis, University of London.

STERN, H. H. (1960). *Parent Education: An International Survey*. Hull: University of Hull Institute of Education with UNESCO Institute for Education, Hamburg.

WHITE PAPER (1978). *Violence to Children*, Cmnd 7123. London: HMSO.

WHITFIELD, R. C. (1978). 'Choice within a National Framework for the School Curriculum' in *Westminster Studies in Education*, 1, pp. 63-72.

WHITFIELD, R. C. (ed.) (1971). *Disciplines of the Curriculum*. New York and Maidenhead: McGraw-Hill.

# CHAPTER 6

Towards Social Policies
for Families

Professor Sir J.C. Spence, a biologist by training and a Professor of
Child Care, in the record of the first NCH Convocation Lecture in
1946 on 'The Purpose of the Family' wrote:

> . . . it is within the bounds of possibility that our civilisation will
> decline through a failure to preserve and promote family life and
> the neighbouring society in which it should be set.

He believed that the attitude of the State was crucial. While up to the
Second World War the State had always been a supporter of family
rights, making only minimal and necessary encroachments upon
parental authority and upon family feeling, Spence warned that if
administrative and political power became vested too much in the
hands of people inexperienced in family life, with a political
philosophy based exclusively upon economic theory, then they might
not foresee that the newly created social instruments, such as nurseries,
nursery schools and community centres could harm the family.
Somewhat prophetically he went on to say:

> We of this generation, through the decline of the family, are
> witnessing the most sudden biological change the human race has
> known. The dangers of this sudden change are intensified by the
> decline of neighbourliness, by the encroachments of State in-
> stitutions on the family and by the spread of a materialistic
> individualism. The complexity of modern society commits us to an
> increasing arrangement of our lives by the State. Anglo-Saxon
> civilisation will decline unless people recreate natural
> neighbourliness, and unless the State bases its actions on a
> philosophy of human welfare which recognises that the unit of
> society is not the isolated individual but the family. To that end, the
> function and the purpose of the family must be known and realised,
> and our social legislation, our methods of education, our spon-
> taneous mutual aid, and our public spending of money must be
> adjusted to that purpose.

And all that was said before we created high rise council flats and the new towns, before social and economic forces tempted both parents out of the home to paid employment, and before social affairs were legislated more in favour of adult gratification than sufficiently towards the rights and needs of children.

Now as some of the inevitable failings of the welfare state in our liberal democracy come to light, perhaps more as a result of human nature than simply resource shortage or maladministration, there is a belated if presently muted upsurge of academic and professional interest in 'family policy', which may yet come to the forefront of concern among politicians. Whatever our plans and policies for education for parenthood, they will make little real impression upon our needs in prevention unless they are devised within a wider framework of factors which impinge directly on families—population control, employment, housing, transport, taxation and economic benefits. Whether we like it or not, these set limits to the quality of child care and parental well-being, no matter how well-informed and sensitively caring are the parents.

In Chapter 5 we have noted the present state of the craft of EFP and some of its historical roots. Some of the stimulus to expand school course provision in child development has undoubtedly arisen from teachers' convictions about the need to avoid the transmission of human deficiencies resulting from experience from one generation to another. Whilst this motive is understandable and has recognisable foundations, influences other than the educational or genetic also contribute significantly to child well-being. It behoves all of us who are concerned with EFP to see the topic in a fuller context, and not to imply that it can ever be a cure-all in the absence of complementary economic and social change. Figure 7 is an attempt to map some of the fundamental causal and interactive relationships for EFP in its broader structural frame (see page 104).

In this chapter some essentially non-educational factors are briefly referred to which affect the lives of growing children and their parents, if only to emphasise that educational action, of whatever kind, spawned in isolation, is bound to have severely restricted impact.

## THE NATURE OF FAMILY POLICY

Broadly defined, family policy encompasses everything that government does to and for the family. However, this includes not only

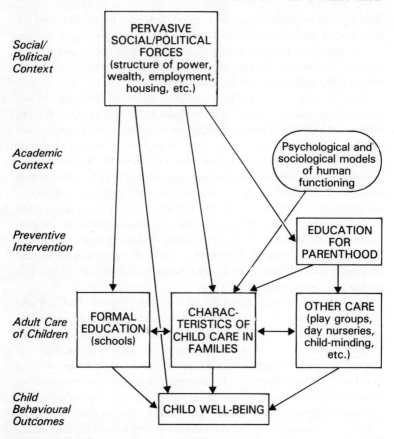

*Social/*
*Political*
*Context*

PERVASIVE
SOCIAL/POLITICAL
FORCES
(structure of power,
wealth, employment,
housing, etc.)

*Academic*
*Context*

Psychological and
sociological models
of human
functioning

*Preventive*
*Intervention*

EDUCATION
FOR
PARENTHOOD

*Adult Care*
*of Children*

FORMAL
EDUCATION
(schools)

CHARAC-
TERISTICS OF
CHILD CARE IN
FAMILIES

OTHER CARE
(play groups,
day nurseries,
child-minding,
etc.)

*Child*
*Behavioural*
*Outcomes*

CHILD WELL-BEING

7   *A chart placing Education for Parenthood in context*

directly articulated explicit policies, such as maternity and child
benefits, in which families are the object of concern, but also, and
possibly more crucially, the indirect and often unforeseen consequences upon families of other governmental actions, such as the siting
of industries and the devising of trading regulations. In the UK, a
country which has been classified by Kamerman and Kahn as one
with only 'implicit' and 'reluctant' family policies, the pervasiveness of
government activity upon families can tend to go unrecognised. In
such situations there is no ready-made political watchdog, such as a
Ministry for the Family, to chart and anticipate derived side-effects
which could undermine family well-being.

We noted in Chapter 3 the diversity of family types: two parents married or cohabiting, one parent divorced or separated or widowed or unmarried, relatives or guardians caring for children, and so on. In these the only common factor is at least one adult and one child. The field of family policy is thus a surrogate for 'policies for families'—a range of provisions for a range of circumstances in which children are involved. It includes the prevention of direct daily dependency on others, particularly for children, women, the elderly and the handicapped. In some countries family policy has been used as a vehicle for achieving broader goals such as political indoctrination, counter-acting inequality and labour market control. Since in this text no narrow definition of family has been employed, 'family policy' can be viewed as a criterion for social policy choice, in the sense of what impact on family life does or will a given social policy have. As such there may be few policy arenas in which it is not relevant, from, for example, family planning to land utilisation. Family well-being, whatever its constituents, thus becomes a criterion for decision-making and assessing the consequences of public policies generally.

It is presumably fundamentally the need to recognise this criterion which has recently brought together some 40 voluntary agencies to discuss the setting up of a possible 'Family Forum'. This body would have wide representation from trade unions, employers, political parties, ethnic minorities, parents' groups, religious bodies, charities, and so on, and would stimulate the recognition of family considerations in the formation of social policy as a whole. This kind of contemporary concern, which reflects a loss of confidence in education and a reduced faith in politics as well as a recognition of the need for overall coordination, is however not confined to the UK. Most countries continue to view the family as the central institution for the economic support, nurture, care and socialising of children, and as unlikely to be widely replaced in that role. The changes in family structure and composition, and of family function and roles, some of which were outlined in Chapter 4, are reflected in many other developed countries, and the family is thus emerging as a symbol in an effort to frame a communal, rather than an individualistic, view of social policy.

The evidence of the significant disintegration of traditional family forms marshalled in Chapter 3 to underline the undeniable defects in the net of contemporary child care may, it is conceded, be balanced by a less alarmist view. Adults may be shifting form and function within their families in response to external social changes and their relatively new-found freedoms for conscious choice, facilitated by, for example, developments in contraception, the fresh momentum within the women's movement, and the liberalisation of divorce and property law. This may be fine for some of those adults, determined not to let anything get between them and their satisfactions, but if it is specific partners rather than family commitments which are often being rejected, then many children tend to be on the losing end, with sometimes little direct protection for them even from the State during the possible transition period. It may not be long, however, before differences in value and perspective between those responsible for caring for children, and those who are not, take on real political significance. The development of family policies is by no means guaranteed, since many adults could well become impatient with children and their problems: parenthood and even teaching the young are no longer considered the most honourable of callings. Further-more, it must be noted that those interested in policies for families by no means share the same motives; disparate interest groups may support the same policy for different reasons. Feminists, for example, press for sexual equality, maternity benefits and substitute child care, while traditionalists view family policy as a means of securing the *status quo* or indeed reversing recent trends. Some tenable mid-point might be to recognise that the family is resilient, adaptable and here to stay, and now requires a framework of government which is more respon-sive to its needs. Hence the scenario of family policy must include educational support, employment provision, housing, child care and health services, recognition in the tax system, and other forms of attention to the needs of families. If this can be set within a broad framework of sensitive population monitoring based upon multiple projections of the numbers of people of different age groups which the total resources of a nation might support under humane and viable conditions, then so much the better.

Unlike a number of European countries, Britain has never had a government minister for the family, nor indeed one for population. Consequently, and not surprisingly, there has never been a coord-inated range of social policies for families, even though assumptions about responsibilities and dependencies among parents and children, derivative from Judao-Christian traditions, have undoubtedly under-pinned much social legislation. Even today, notwithstanding the upsurge of interest in family policy, neither of the two main political parties holds any brief for initiating a minister for the family, despite their shared wish that public policies should strengthen rather than weaken family life. On both sides of the House of Commons there is a reticence to 'interfere' directly in family life, to invade its intimacy and privacy. While it may be the case that 'it is people, not politicians, who determine the success of family life', to quote Patrick Jenkin, at the time of writing Secretary of State for Social Services, there is a reluctance to recognise the restricted room for manoeuvre which is possessed by ordinary families as a result of the activities of the State. The fact must be faced that the insularity, privacy and independence of the family is now, and perhaps always has been, an illusion. Family life is in part private and in part public, and to regard a man's relations with his wife, his employment status, his tax benefits, the way in which he plays with his children, and the costs of the child's school uniform as all part of the same piece is to deny social and political reality. The real issue for child care now is whether Government is prepared to enter into genuine partnership with parents and other caregivers, regularising and coordinating policy, or whether to leave an untidy patchwork of segregated public and private efforts.

EMPLOYMENT AND THE FAMILY

On pages 38–41 the large increase in the proportion of women who both have the care of children and go out to work was discussed, with all the attendant problems of child care which that involves, assuming, as in most cases, that the father in the two-parent family is also in employment. Clearly members of families need employment as a means of income, for variety of activity and stimulation, and for personal dignity, so that there is a feeling of making a productive contribution to the nation's life rather than being totally dependent upon welfare benefits provided indirectly by those who are employed. However, the right of mothers and fathers each to work full-time has now become open to question from both the perspectives of child care and employment availability.

Increasing structural unemployment is now regarded as inevitable for the rest of this century unless some fundamental changes are made in policy and attitudes. It is widely recognised that upturns in business confidence, investment and world trade will periodically reduce unemployment, but will not cure the essential structural weaknesses arising from technological innovation and changed social patterns of employment. Young adults are over the next two decades likely to be the most affected in this new situation, and this is likely to lead to significant social unrest and tension within and between generations— between those with work and those without it. Whatever else, we have a major problem in reaching the next century without severe dis-locations in social life in order to be in a position to achieve a gradual transition to the haven and alleged benefits of the 'post-industrial society'. Assuming that technological advances will continue to displace labour, and that the right of access to work will remain a predominant ethic, the problem rests essentially in devising social mechanisms for a more democratic sharing of the work which is available. Structural unemployment thus fundamentally demands a change in our social values; changes in investment, productivity, turn-over and profits, while important, are secondary considerations in anything other than the short term.

For the majority there is not one but *two* locations where 'work' is done—the home and the external, paid situation—though as we have noted, work at home as a parent is left out of the majority of socio-economic equations. Because it has not been economically valued, parenthood and 'housework' have become low-status occupations with, as we have seen earlier, some widespread and tragic social and educational consequences. The 'production' of well-adjusted and competent youngsters—the seed corn of the future—through the devotion of time, care and concern of parents is, we have implied, no less important than the production of visible and invisible goods for export. Indeed it may be argued that parenthood is a *more* intrinsically worthwhile activity than employment in industrial manufacture and trade, that is, anything except primary production.

Parents nevertheless remain the most cost-effective social service for children's well-being, regardless of moral or religious traditions. We have seen that in the decade 1961–71 an extra 1.5 million married women joined the nation's payroll external to the home—a number almost equivalent to those persons unemployed during the late 1970s. To put this statistic in more appropriate non-sexist contem-porary terms, over 2 million married couples have since the last war increased their corporate share of the work external to the home that is available. Already, and certainly in the future, this acquisition denies appropriate access to paid employment among the young, and furthermore decreases the time, care and attention that can be given by parents to childrearing. If we include the tasks of parenthood in the total work equation, then there is more than enough work to go round for everyone; the problem rests in the devising of means to redistribute it more appropriately through a more sensitive understanding of the rights of all sections of the population—men, women, youth, *and* those without an effective voice: children.

Most discussions of work-sharing centre on the reduction of the standard working week and/or of overtime. In recent years the reduction of the former has usually been used in wage bargaining as an indirect means for increasing the latter, and thus the total value of take home pay of those who have work. Recent legislation regarding job tenure has had the undesirable effect of encouraging employers to make do with their existing work-force, making overtime available as demand dictates, rather than risk hiring new staff. Again, this is fine for those who have work, but not for those who have not.

But there is another possibility regarding work sharing which family policy might take on board. Might we consider restricting each nuclear family with children under the age of sixteen to a maximum of, say, 1.5 full-time external job-equivalents? The legislation required for such a non-sexist social policy should not be too different in kind from that required to limit overtime, which appears to be something which the trade unions are prepared to consider, if only in theory at present. Such a policy would raise the status of parenthood, and, if accompanied by more adequate and extensive educational and economic support for families, would improve the quality of care given to children in the pre-school and school years, leading to better life adjustment and educational achievement. While it might curtail the liberty of some parents, it would be likely to increase and widen the framework of responsibility surrounding the decisions of getting married, obtaining formal employment and having children. It would take some of the stress out of coping with the demands of two jobs each for mothers and fathers. It would look at the family, rather than the individual, as the unit of social planning, from the perspectives of both employment and child care. These two domains, which are so important in the daily lives of all families, are rarely linked in our social thinking, partly due to the differing government departments involved, and partly because we allow commercial and industrial considerations in the arrangement of work schedules to predominate over family considerations. For example, most mothers and fathers are likely to have little consideration given by their employers to their family circumstances in the arrangement of their working hours; production lines and office hours are usually not in the least family-centred.

Certainly, child care considerations apart, we cannot now turn a blind eye to the spectre of a projected 4 million unemployed in Britain by the mid 1980s; nor are young adults between the ages of seventeen and 25 likely to tolerate the 25% unemployment level forecast for them by the EEC. The use of the family unit as something of a regulator in these impending circumstances might indeed turn out to be the most democratic solution for the community as a whole.

## FAMILY INCOME: BENEFITS AND TAXATION

It took the best part of twenty years before the case for centrally distributed family allowances, pressed by Eleanor Rathbone, reached the UK statute book under Sir William Beveridge's guidance in 1942. The recognition that not all men were heads of families, that not all families were of the same size, having an equal number of dependants, and that a single, usually male, wage could not necessarily provide on its own for the whole of the family's needs for all of the time, was certainly not instant. Even under a socialist administration, the by no means generous revisions to the scheme of child benefits were agreed in 1976 only after considerable political manoeuvreing and press manipulation. Many of the benefits of the welfare state are dependent upon a prosperous economy and high employment rates. Nevertheless, despite the swings of the economy, the historical record of tax and benefit support for families is not good. The *peak* postwar year for family income support was 1955, and Table 15 compares this with present levels subsequent to the recent introduction of the child benefit

*Table 15*

*Value of child allowances to a basic rate taxpayer at April 1979 prices*

| Year | 1 child | 2 children | 3 children | 4 children |
|------|---------|-----------|-----------|-----------|
| 1955 | £4.19 | £9.58 | £15.09 | £20.52 |
| 1979 | £4.00* | £8.00 | £12.00 | £16.00 |

* Frugal minimal budgets per child were estimated (1979) by the Child Poverty Action Group at £6.86 per week for a two-year-old and £10.08 for an eleven-year-old.

scheme which has replaced the older family allowances plus child allowances on the Pay As You Earn taxcodes. If the recent years of high inflation on essential goods for families (food, housing, clothing, energy and transport) are taken into account, the figures are very depressing in terms of economic policies for families, especially as, at the time of writing, no increases are imminent.

While family poverty is difficult to define, the thresholds of earned income below which supplementary benefits become payable attempt to define the minimum for viable living. While many experts believe these levels to be inadequate, half a million British children were living below this semi-official poverty line in 1976, while a further 4 million were within 40% of it, in so-called 'marginal poverty'. In many cases the wife's earnings are vital in keeping the family out of poverty. The DHSS in 1971 estimated that the number of poor two-parent families would have trebled without the assistance of mothers' earnings in supplementing those of employed fathers. It is believed by many commentators that family poverty is consistently underestimated, and certainly one of the oddities of the new child benefit scheme is that it takes no account of the age of the child. What parent would have devised a scheme of financial support for families which distributes the same for a baby of fifteen weeks as it does for an adolescent of fifteen years, who tends to cost as much to transport as an adult, and probably more than an adult to feed and clothe? The old system of tax allowances may have been unfair in that it was of more benefit to those with the highest incomes, but at least it did slightly acknowledge the dramatic increase in the financial burden represented by children as they grow older.

Relative to pensioners, traditionally an underprivileged group, contemporary economic observers believe that families have fared badly in recent years. Certainly no one can pretend that the following minimum weekly income benefits provide each group with the same standard of living:

|     |                                                      | 1976    | 1980    |
| --- | ---------------------------------------------------- | ------- | ------- |
| (a) | pensioner couple                                     | £24.85  | £37.65  |
| (b) | husband, pregnant wife and two children aged 4 and 6 | £28.60  | £43.29  |
| (c) | mother, father and two teenage sons aged 13 and 15   | £33.65  | £48.40  |

Hence the concept of fiscal planning for family budgets which vary throughout the family life cycle has been suggested. In this computer age, it should not be beyond our capability to administer the appropriate ground rules for state-aided family budgets, separately programmed for each family over time. A great deal of pressure on wages and salaries arises from the needs of parents trying to cope with the heavy economic demands of parenthood, especially in early middle age, and this must be a factor affecting industrial relations. One recent estimate suggested that some £13,000 million should be re-distributed to families as the measure of post-war fiscal neglect; this corresponds to almost 20% of total annual government expenditure and would provide an equivalent of close to £20 per week for each child. This is perhaps somewhat extravagant, even with present price levels. Nevertheless, to treble the existing child benefits would reflect more accurately the real costs of childrearing. One of Beveridge's implicit principles, which has yet to be reflected in policy, was to pay cash allowances high enough to meet the subsistence costs of each child, irrespective of the employment or marital status of the parents. More realistic levels of child benefit could be effectively re-christened as 'wages' for child care, whether received by father or mother or both in response to their pledge to give close to full-time home-based care.

Of course these issues are politically and economically controversial, but the Marxist principle of 'from each according to his abilities, to each according to his needs' still has merit for guiding fiscal policy in a caring society, even though 'abilities' and 'needs' are complex to define. Is there anything intrinsically unfair in the idea that single employees and couples without dependent children should in effect subsidise those with others to care for? It seems not, at least in principle, for state education and existing child benefits are examples of its practice. The crux of the issue is the *extent* to which we perceive overall child care as a social as well as parental responsibility, and furthermore are prepared to act upon any righteous unease by providing adequate and properly coordinated family income supports.

Within families too there is still resistance to direct government transfers from 'wallet to purse', which is what the new child benefit scheme has achieved, despite the 1976 opposition from some male-dominated trade unions. Surveys have shown that pay rises are not necessarily fairly shared within families, and the pooling of total family resources cannot be assumed. The source of finance and the person to whom the payments are first made still matter, for our social security and income tax systems still reflect persistent assumptions about the unequal economic relations between husbands and wives, and about their division of labour in the family. Indeed, the systems implicitly reinforce the male duty to participate in the labour market, leaving where possible the female in the caregiving role with respect to her husband, the children and any sick or elderly relatives who may live near at hand or in the family home.

Economic policies for families, perhaps unfortunately, have been dominated by a divisive concern for poor families as a sub-group rather than families as a whole. This has left the family lobby politically rather impotent, and many middle-class families do not fully appreciate their own stresses and sacrifices in childrearing partly caused by inadequate income redistribution in favour of families. A decade ago Margaret Wynn wrote tellingly about the way in which, without formal family policies, economic forces evolve and develop adversely for the interests of families with dependent children. One of her conclusions was that:

> The progress of communities is, in consequence, retarded by the poverty of the environment of most children even in the more advanced Western countries.

A similar burden is conveyed by the more recent and important reports from the Carnegie Council on Children and the National Academy of Sciences in the USA.

We must be in part concerned with the long-term transfer of resources towards investment in future generations, rather than allowing family concerns to be threatened by the pressures and conditioned temptations of immediate consumption and short-term expediency. With the many improvements in contraceptive practice and developing social norms, as well as the suggested education for parenthood, fear of overpopulation need not hold us back from adequate provision for family welfare. The child benefit scheme is a major step forward in recognising children as individuals, for the first child was never counted for the former family allowances, but Treasury advisers still 'steal' from families, perhaps because they have no direct experience of what it is like to struggle to make ends meet with a growing family on a single income. A first plank in building an *explicit* national family policy will be for government departments to organise their intelligence and outlook in family cycle terms as a basis for reflective and informed policy-making. Unless the economy of the family, like that of the nation, is strong, everything else of value becomes akin to pushing water up hill. The nation cannot *expect* appropriate parental responsibility without assisting the family's economic foundations much more extensively than at present. Regrettably, little has changed the response and actions of either major political party since Wynn laid out a case for all to see.

## HOUSING AND COMMUNITY FACILITIES

Further facets of the total social context which provide conditions for effective child care and complementary familial stability are the housing in which families reside and their neighbouring community facilities. It has been remarked that we, or more strictly, the architectural profession and the planners and the building regulations and accommodation guidelines shape our buildings; then the buildings shape us. Patterns of home design over past decades clearly influence childrearing practices and social interaction in families. It is certainly questionable whether architects and planning authorities have often considered the social consequences of housing design, whether inside each home or within the community collective. Successive waves of council and speculative building for families have been motivated too much by a 'roofs over heads at minimal unit cost' philosophy rather than an acquaintance with the desired lifestyles of the eventual occupants and their kin. Similar insensitivities have occurred in school design. The 'high-rise' phase most obviously demonstrates lack of concern for both young families and the elderly, and preoccupation with nuclear families upon the part of planners has rarely enabled the old to stay near their kin, while at the same time families are blamed for not caring for their elderly relatives.

Design and planning is one part of family housing issues; availability and finance are the others. Two thirds of the British housing market rest within the private sector of owner-occupiers and landlords. Here no particular priority is given to families with children; the ability to purchase, irrespective of social circumstance, is the dominating criterion, and for most this involves appropriate mortgage arrangements. The young couple's chance of obtaining a mortgage for their desired style of property may well be increased by their not having young children, thus allowing them both to work full-time. The escalating costs of housing in relation to incomes make entry into the owner-occupier housing market a huge problem for young marrieds, let alone the couple or single persons with dependants. Discrimination against families with children within the privately rented sector is frequent, save at the cheapest and most expensive ends of the market, for children can be perceived as a social nuisance, and single room rentals are often more profitable to landlords. Public housing policy on the other hand has traditionally given priority to families, but the demographic history of much council housing is now causing concern. Because there is a somewhat uniform age and range of household types on many estates, this leads to a lack of variety in community socialising and of people willing to and capable of taking their proper share of responsibility in community affairs. If there is any discrimination in the public authority sector, it tends to go against the one-parent family, the large family and the three-generation family, owing to a combination of residence qualifications and the type of property available; only 3% of post-war council housing has four or more bedrooms, for example. Although housing amenities have undoubtedly improved in the post-war years, a recent National Child Development Study estimate suggested that at least one in five children had nevertheless experienced an overcrowded home (greater than 1.5 persons per room), and/or housing lacking basic facilities of a bathroom, hot water and an indoor lavatory by the time they left school in 1974.

Over recent years there has been a growing awareness that increased social mobility and changes of lifestyle require positive steps in order to maintain or regenerate community spirit and community activities. This applies particularly in urban and suburban areas, though rural community activities are these days by no means self-perpetuating. Modern styles of life, in which the private motor car and the television are perhaps the most significant influences, have tended to shut in family groups more among themselves. This often leaves community leaders with consequent difficulties of overcoming apathy, of regaining communication and a natural neighbourliness in which skills and interests are shared.

The building of community halls and sports and leisure centres to complement libraries, schools and church facilities has been a wise investment, though in many areas these facilities could still be used much more imaginatively for the sake of parents and children. Restrictions often still apply which forbid the use of vacant community premises at certain times of day and for certain groups of people. There is for example no fundamental reason why 'latchkey children' could not be allowed to stay for relaxing activities on school premises under a different kind of non-teacher supervision until one or other parent can collect them, though the Gingerbread organisation for one-parent families, for example, prefers other kinds of premises, if they are available, of an 'open house' style. In some areas the creation of family and community centres which gather together under one roof a wide range of activities—library, daycare nurseries, general medical, dental and social services, sports and other leisure amenities—seems to have been very beneficial. These are, at the moment, a sparse feature in most regions, and require both significant capital investment and a willingness among diverse interest groups to work together; all this can take lengthy negotiation subsequent to the vision to create a new community focus.

The potential effects of community activities upon youngsters as they grow up should certainly not be minimised. Within social activities outside the family, children can grow to appreciate the meaning and purpose of other kinds of coherent groups. Further learning through other, in their eyes significant, adults who are not perceived directly as teachers or custodians, and who will often be volunteers (for example, in the scouting movement), is crucial in the widening of children's social and moral development. Perhaps what is needed most in many areas is the opportunity for whole families to do things together with other whole families, rather than the often too exclusive segregation across families by age and sex. Here churches and schools have a part to play. The Plowden Report in 1967 summed up the need cogently: 'It has been recognised that education is concerned with the whole man; henceforth it must be concerned with the whole family.'

That families live in groups and need each other will always remain a foundation stone of issues pertinent to child care. The crucial task within community education, community regeneration and maintenance is to utilise the public services as catalysts to encourage voluntary endeavours, and particularly those which assist children and their caregivers to lead richer lives.


## PROFESSIONAL SERVICES AND THE FAMILY

On both sides of the Atlantic the difficulties of raising a family in contemporary society are now being increasingly recognised.

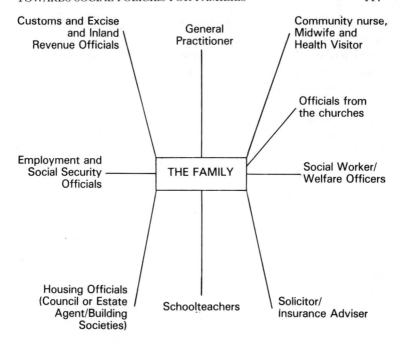

Customs and Excise and Inland Revenue Officials

General Practitioner

Community nurse, Midwife and Health Visitor

Officials from the churches

Employment and Social Security Officials — THE FAMILY

Social Worker/ Welfare Officers

Housing Officials (Council or Estate Agent/Building Societies)

Schoolteachers

Solicitor/ Insurance Adviser

8   *Professional personnel impinging on the family*

However the efforts being made by parents amid the difficulties are becoming more respected in the academic and professional literature than was the case some years ago. Many of those working alongside families are at long last realising that their interventions, however skilled and well-meaning, can only treat symptons; solving fundamental family problems is only possible with the full cooperation of parents. All family-relevant professionals—and there are plenty of them (see Figure 8)—and politicians do well to heed D.W. Winnicott's advice of 1944: 'Whatever does not specifically back up the idea that parents are responsible people will in the long run be harmful to the very core of society.'

The aims and activities of EFP, as was emphasised in the previous chapter, are concerned fundamentally with fostering parental confidence, awareness, competence, and thereby responsibility, by building upon their covert and inborn desire to succeed in rearing their children through the use of professionals to enhance their capacities for self-help. It is surely not beyond our wit to redirect some of the efforts of professionals towards client confidence-building. The social need is now in any case too great to tackle the range of problems solely by the curatives of expensive professionals, and professional help must in the end become self-defeating if it undermines and destroys, however subtly, the dignity of the clients. Some extreme commentators, such as Christopher Lasch, suggest somewhat unfairly that the family is in a state of collapse as a result of the intrusion of professionals. Perhaps this may be true in some cases, though in others the professional services are too stretched to be able to hear and respond to some of the cries for help.

Nevertheless, the onward march of professional groups continues, bolstered by specific combinations of educational credits, certification and membership of professional associations. These confer status and tend to both mystify and make private essential knowledge and skills, causing in their wake no small organisational problems for central and local government administrators. Professionalisation has happened too much in teaching despite the fact that we all have something to teach; it is happening in social work despite the fact that we can all help; and, following its earlier establishment in the USA, it seems likely to happen in counselling despite the fact that we can all lend a confidential friendly ear to a neighbour in trouble. With declining school rolls and the release of classroom space for possible use in much needed extensions to pre-school services, we might predict the further professionalisation of the early childhood educators—anxious for parental involvement, yes, provided its limits are controlled. So if we are not careful we may be incrementally lulled into feeling that some professional exists somewhere for every problem, that we each have a strictly restricted sphere of operation which we jealously guard, that Big Brother has sorted out all the demarcation disputes, and that even the good Samaritan has to be trained. Whither human dignity?

Nevertheless at the other extreme the professions must not be outlawed, for families do need support; and they need it now, as the play of market forces and the resulting inequalities outstrip the present abilities of many parents to cope. Concurrently, however, there is the wish of many to participate rather than to remain passive receptors of services paid for through taxes and rates levied on them. The era of unchallenged neutral professional expertise bestowed by the meritocracy is probably nearing its conclusion as responsible consumerism grows. The demand for educational accountability and the unease with present arrangements for school government are probably the first major examples of this. It is already clear that schools and their staffs will not in future have the same unfettered right to determine their own destinies as some have claimed in the past; nor will it be possible to use traditional parent/teacher association activities as a camouflage for genuine participation.

Into the 1980s it seems likely that we will see a slow renegotiation of territories between public and professionals, with the family at the centre of some of the inevitable skirmishing. But the professionals must not play their cards with too much arrogance if they are both to maintain their integrity and have their licence to practise by the community ratified through the political and fiscal mechanisms; teachers and some health service workers, for example, have in recent times gone close to losing public credibility and sympathy. The laity are no longer the abject, illiterate poor, but the political nation created by social and educational amelioration over a century. It is they who by their decisions and taxes create and sustain the services they require, however distant their influence sometimes seems; professionals certainly must not be perceived as conspiring against them.

Suspicions about some elements of professionalism may be long overdue, but simply to dilute existing services or to dismantle them without adequately thought-out alternatives would be lunacy. The challenge is to devise contexts in which families, informed through education, may be offered more choices about the kinds of help they need, from professionals, volunteers, or simply good neighbours. A fresh climate is required in which families can work out new and less hierarchical alliances with helping and catalytic professionals, whose training and expertise can avowedly contribute to improving the quality of life for parents and children alike.

## EDUCATION OR INCOME OR SERVICES? OR ALL THREE?

The need for more integrated social planning is undoubtedly an important lesson of the 1970s and a top priority for the 1980s. Government has not hitherto defined social objectives in any detail, and even in outline they are not related to the functions of administrative departments and other agencies. Despite the work of the Government 'think tank' (Central Policy Review Staff) on a joint approach to (later, a 'framework for') social policy, there is still not apparatus to control and monitor social planning and to modify the management of the economy with social and family aims in view. But much of the preparatory groundwork in political science, social administration and educational research has yet to be done so that we can understand more about our attitudes towards the family and the reasons for failure in existing provision. Ordinary families, rather than the more obviously deprived ones, have been taken for granted and have rarely been the topic of research, let alone the unit of concern for policy.

Despite the severe limitations of educational initiatives devised in isolation from the social and economic context, it is a major contention of this text that even with relatively low unemployment, economic boom, and the provision of still more adequate and comprehensive professional services (each of which at present looks unrealistic) there is absolutely no way in which the adequate care of children from cradle to adulthood can be ensured without the informed cooperation and commitment of parents, parents-to-be and other significant adults. Our willingness to cooperate and motivation to dedicate our time, energy and resources to child care can derive in part from our innate desire to protect our young, which we share with others in the animal kingdom. But within contemporary society we have all been conditioned to some extent to assume that others will or should care, while we get on with seeking our own adult satisfactions which need not touch too closely the lives of our children. The products of an age of secular faith and political indeterminancy, many of us are nonetheless looking for personal commitments at a time when the traditional notions of marriage and career are being reworked. Few have mastered the demands of multiple roles and multiple careers, and yet the need for commitment haunts us, as does the vision of a better world. 'What is *my* commitment (for it is personal for each of us) to work, to other persons, to children?' is the question which lingers on and will not go away.

Our attitudes towards parenthood and child care, and our lifestyles, are unlikely to be shifted in favour of children unless we become better informed as a community about child care and development, and thereby come to a more sensitive understanding about what constitute children's rights and what our complementary obligations should be. That is an educational matter and the prime task for education for parenthood, with preparation for parenthood being the focus of primary prevention and parent education being a foundation for the cost-effective utilisation of a range of necessary support services. Despite some encouraging innovations, we have barely begun the educational tasks, and, even among advocates and enthusiastic practitioners, the size and complexity of the exercise is probably not appreciated.

Whatever else is done by way of shorter-term measures, we neglect the long-term educational investment at the community's peril. The recent important reports from the Carnegie Commission on Children and the National Academy of Sciences in the USA, referred to earlier, view child care as an important and legitimate form of work, and though they have relevance to the policy debate in Britain, include little reference to education, as if resigned to a defeatist position regarding teaching and learning, believing that jobs, income and housing are all that really matter. Both these reports stress an income strategy for child care and parental well-being, and do not concurrently examine the efficacy of the various support services. Whilst the vision of lasting reform simply through expanded opportunity is attenuated, the redistribution of income remains too facile a solution to a complex array of problems. On both sides of the Atlantic, the prevalence of economists in policy debates blinkers vision—a curious phenomenon, considering their inability to solve problems more strictly in their own domain, such as inflation and unemployment.

Of course families need money, income needs redistributing more in accordance with the real costs of childrearing, and we may still need the extremes of inequality of opportunity overcome before the professional support services can make adequate impact across the board, but the underlying market model of competitive self-interest, of switching income to make the disadvantaged more competitive, is fundamentally flawed, certainly from a moral perspective. The need for income and jobs is self-evident; the need for public knowledge, understanding and compassion probably less so in our atomistic society. Our social, health and educational services may be inefficient, but to sidestep the agonies of their improvement through communal action by concentrating upon overtly economic solutions would be both naive and empty. In reality there is no tidy distinction between educational or income or service strategies, and all three must be kept aligned on any tenable policy map.

At the heart of the policy issue lies the challenge to build communal bridges between classes and generations, between the rich and the

poor, and between minorities and majorities, between professionals
and the families to whom they minister, between those with children to
care for and those without such immediate responsibilities. These
bridges could constitute new alliances for collective action and mutual
fulfilment without which social policy propositions become barren and
perhaps even dangerous. There can be no retreat into the privacy of
individual households if we are to find answers to our collective
political problems which a focus on family matters instantly reveals.
While much of the drama of family life, its joys, its successes, its
tragedies and its pains, will be experienced within the confines of the
household, or perhaps shared with at least the neighbours next door,
caring public policy could help parents and children to meet the ups
and downs with more confidence, security and dignity. No family,
even the most wealthy, is self-sufficient; all need knowledge and
services at one time or another, and when they do, it is rarely the result
of blatant moral deficiency.

 Whatever else happens to family policy, we must see that education,
income and services are *collectively* included in the discussion. At the
same time, individual needs must be respected without prejudice,
within what Spence called an 'atmosphere of natural neighbourliness'.
A social movement with concern for the family is afoot and is more
than the sum of the idiosyncrasies of those who make it up. The
family's concerns are the concerns of the community as a whole. Over
50 years ago Eleanor Rathbone, concerned as she was with the
economic status of the family, and of its members in relation to each
other and to other units of which the community is made up, wrote in
*The Disinherited Family* a telling phrase unhampered by some of the
fetishes of modern economics:

> . . . the family is after all the institution that matters most. It is at
> once indispensable as a means to all the rest and, in a sense, an end
> in itself. Pluck from under the family all the props which religion
> and morality have given it, strip it of the glamour, true or false, cast
> round it by romance, it will still remain a prosaic, indisputable fact,
> that the whole business of begetting, bearing and rearing children,
> is the most essential of the nation's business.

A 'Family Forum', a statutory 'Family Commission' or a 'Ministry
for the Family' may not be the most appropriate institutional
mechanism for promoting serious rather than *ad hoc* social policies for
families. Maybe the tasks can be accomplished through new kinds of
cooperation between existing government departments. Many would

fear, and rightly, the development of a new family bureaucracy. What is clear, however, is that new initiatives are needed, and urgently. If that political fact can be recognised, then there are many people capable of discussing sensible administrative arrangements through which the initial educational, social and fiscal details can be worked out and new impacts made upon practice.

## AN EDUCATIONAL RATHER THAN MEDICAL MODEL

Although the term 'prevention' has occurred frequently throughout this text, it must not be deduced that intervention is being suggested upon the basis of a simple curative medical analogy of an assumed disease pathology, expert diagnosis, remedial prescription, and expected cure. Nor indeed is the preventive medical counterpart of eradication of the causative agent, immunisation, and positive health measures entirely appropriate either. The field of family matters and child care is too complex to respond to that analysis, as Figure 7 (page 104) has depicted. The educational model which has been outlined begins from where people are, and is one in which information or help is given and, if appropriate, change determined, through collaborative dialogue rather than through prescriptions for a wide range of pre-classified deficits and deviations. First aid, crucial though it often is, is no substitute for long-term preventive policies which take account of the total cultural environment. Explaining behaviour solely or chiefly in terms of individual pathology, or family pathology, or even local community pathology, without taking into account the wider socio-economic and educational forces simply will not suffice.

Medical models, albeit sometimes used by educators, tend to produce linear modes of action, whereas an educational model, at its best, takes into account that the causes of social events are both complex and dynamic. This means that a flexible stance is required if the necessary committed cooperation of the clients with all their varied needs is to be obtained. The growth of parental competence cannot depend solely upon particular contents of any preparative, supportive or intervention programme. And for the most part we are concerned with habilitation rather than rehabilitation, with promoting individuals' abilities to understand and to adjust to changing circumstances, rather than retrospectively compensating them for their lack of some elusive idealised status or style of life.

So interventions must be long-term, and sensitively geared to the needs of individual families whose dynamics and ideologies must be understood, and not denigrated from beyond the touchlines of their daily reality. Consultation and partnership are the keys to ethically justified social interventions. Furthermore, there is now widespread experience internationally that pre-school programmes are only likely to lead to long-term benefits, including gains in children's intellectual and socio-emotional development, if genuine parental involvement is secured, and partnerships and frameworks for succession are established. Perhaps the concept of community education, if genuinely one of two-way interaction between laity and professionals, will provide foci for new kinds of extended families and allow the educational philosophies and psychologies of homes and schools to become more permeable and less conflicting. EFP in its varied facets would be a part of such a community programme for all, though quite properly with specific features geared to identified areas and populations. In particular, it would foster adaptive decision-making skills, so that the specific needs of communities at the various stages of their development would be met.

SOCIAL SCIENCE RESEARCH AND POLICY POINTERS FOR CHILD CARE

There is a large gap between most academic social science and public policy chiefly because the relevant research was seldom designed to illuminate policy issues, and 'purist' researchers have rarely been prepared to take the risk of chancing their arm near the periphery of their disciplines where they impinge on one another and the natural settings of human behaviour.* Yet the public credibility of the educational and social sciences depends upon their ability to con-

---

* The Study Commission on the Family, an independent body supported by the Leverhulme Trust, is issuing its first publications in 1980. The Commission's emphasis is on analysing existing material relevant to family policy from a number of academic disciplines. Working parties have been set up to look into the financial circumstances of families, the diversity of family patterns, work and the family, values within the family, and the family and the state. These enquiries should eventually help to forward the cause of family policy in government, industry and the voluntary sector. Such considerations will be able to be placed in an international perspective as a result of an important new project sponsored by the Centre for Educational Research and Innovation of the OECD, 'Family and Education', which will report in 1981.

tribute to improvements in the human condition. At present, in the field of child care and family life, that means making some extrapolations and inferences beyond the empirical data, yet with a keen eye to anticipating unintended consequences of policy options.

Child development research, even if executed on restricted samples of children and on a limited number of dimensions, has revealed a great deal about stages of maturation and the general environmental conditions which promote rather than hinder it. They have, however, indicated little about the optimal social structures for children's well-being. We know that mothers are important caregivers in small nuclear families, but we are relatively ignorant, as was intimated in Chapter 3, about the interactions of fathers and other adults in these or other kinds of families. Few researchers have treated the family network as the unit of investigation, and few if any have looked at the totality of children's life experiences—at home, at play and at school. Hence, for the time being, policy indicators must be derived from the logical consequences of our limited yet significant knowledge, moral principle and a realistic assessment of the arts of the possible. Only Utopia runs according to a perfect theory-based social structure, and our immediate need is to promote social organisations which reflect the knowledge we can respect, despite the errors of measurement and judgment.

The data presented particularly in Chapter 4 were interpreted as suggesting that in Britain we have a growing crisis, or less emotively, at least a problem regarding child care and family life. This problem, in which stability has been exchanged for prosperity, while leaving the unprosperous as disadvantaged as ever, is shared by many other developed countries. Britain and North America, however, seem to be relatively slow at developing overt family policies which might, amid the flux of social life, secure the rights of children more firmly. Necessity might nevertheless stimulate imaginative and effective social policies. It has been the purpose of this book to delineate the form which some of these policies might take. These are now listed in summary form. While these may seem somewhat akin to the manifesto of a 'children and family party', they are presented as being logically derived from our rather restricted understanding of the real needs. Each suggestion seems capable of practical implementation within British society today, given sufficient political will and ethical determination both to face the issues and to give substance to the recent rhetoric of concern for families and children.

1   We need to educate society about the rights of children—that quarter of the population who have no direct political voice—and about the responsibilities of those who have care of them.

2   Every child must become a wanted child. Hence, we need to strengthen the collective awareness of the ethical and practical consequences of procreation, and also encourage reflective application by each couple on their own minimal circumstances which would seem to allow them to enter into parenthood responsibly.

3   In the education service we require a range of policies which have the aim of removing the existing deficiences in child care practice and family membership. Hence the basic core of the somewhat chaotic secondary school curriculum cannot remain immune and must, however organised, include systematic preparation for parenthood for both sexes. At the adult stage a greater variety of educational and practical assistance must be provided which will encourage both fathers and mothers habitually to take advantage of the variety of services available. These must be coordinated and integrated in their provision, whilst the educational system as a whole must relax the formalities of its boundaries for the sake of families.

4   The fiscal system must be used much more aggressively as an instrument of more genuine social justice for families and children. In particular, current child benefit levels should be raised to meet the needs of children and those who care for them now, but with controls which will not encourage the feckless adult and thus prejudice the future.

5   Central government initiatives in family and child care matters must build upon and support existing good practice within statutory and voluntary organisations, rather than create a new bureaucracy, insensitive to local and individual circumstances. The maintenance and regeneration of adequate family and community supports for children should take into account relevant theories of social learning and change.

6   A better coordinated framework of policies affecting families has become urgent. These should include those concerned with the redistribution of wealth and employment, as well as the planning of housing, transport, health measures and education. In short, the basic requirements of contemporary families must be looked at as a whole.

Politicians and professionals of diverse persuasions and skills will need to cooperate in this exercise. The division of responsibilities in family and economic life, between male and female, between parents, community and State, will need to be reassessed. Revised boundaries need to be drawn to meet modern circumstances, taking into account new knowledge relevant to the fulfilment of the rights of children.

It may well be that these policy suggestions, and their origins in the earlier account, will trigger some dissent among sections of those who see themselves as child and family advocates. Yet divisiveness or apathy within the child care community will be one sure guarantee that family policy remains submerged, and compared with, say, defence or even education, relatively unexamined within the government machine. That Government has a crucial role to play in more open consultation and support should not even be a question, for as Margaret Wynn wrote:

> Much social policy, involving the transfer of wealth from families to non-parents, has been examined by small groups of people behind closed doors. Much policy has not been the result of full and adequate consultation . . . nor . . . of thorough investigation.

It is pointless for Government to fear that too much help from the public services may erode a sense of family responsibility, when too little assistance may not make the execution of those responsibilities a practical proposition for sufficient numbers of parents. While the socio-economic context in which we live has been stressed as an important determinant of adult behaviour with respect to child care, individual accountability and conscience within a spectrum of socially possible alternative responses has here also been emphasised.

But there are limitations on government policy, which are partly historical in origin, and which obviously depend crucially upon the health of the national economy. If the task ahead is to raise incrementally the level of awareness of the needs of children and families in society as a whole, and thereby to raise the standards of child care, then conventional central government action alone will not produce the necessary social changes. Professionally at least, though certainly *not* fiscally, government finds it easier to help those who help parents than to help parents directly themselves. Building on this, therefore, government might actively encourage new initiatives, even if this means a change in accounting and financial procedures. Support services for parents, 'drop-in' family resource centres, good neighbour schemes, mass media initiatives, are examples in which further central assistance would be welcomed. Although it is difficult for officials coherently to support local small scale self-help schemes, not least because of their relatively rapid changes in structures and personnel, the example of support to small businesses through quasi-government agencies shows that it can be done. New alliances between government, professionals, communities and caregivers are essential to make for a more child-centred, or more inclusively, person-centred society, in which children and those who care for them will be the beneficiaries.

Family policy presently lies embedded within many contradictory influences in society. Nevertheless, if the family is now a central institution within our social order, and is likely to remain so, then it must be perceived as a key agent both for those who are keen to promote social change, in whatever direction, as well as for those who endeavour to avoid it. Family policy is thus everyone's proper concern, *now*. Failure to develop family policies soon, in the light of the evidence, will place upon the next generation heavy social costs with high moral and financial liabilities.

Nothing can reveal the evidence for one all-human species-hood (and the energies waiting for its universal recognition) as can the endeavour to look at each other's children, their suffering and their miraculous readiness for full human development.

Erik Erikson (1978)

*References*

ADVISORY COMMITTEE ON CHILD DEVELOPMENT (1976). *Towards a National Policy for Children and Families.* Washington, D.C.: National Academy of Sciences.

CENTRAL POLICY REVIEW STAFF (1975). *A Joint Approach to Social Policy.* London: HMSO.

CENTRAL POLICY REVIEW STAFF (1978). *Services for Young Children with Working Mothers.* London: HMSO

COSTIN, L.B. (1979) *Child Welfare: Policies and Practice.* New York: McGraw-Hill.

DEPARTMENT OF EDUCATION AND SCIENCE (1979). *A New Partnership for our Schools.* (The Taylor Report). London: HMSO.

FEATHERSTONE, J. (1979). 'Family Matters' in *Harvard Educational Review*, 49 (1), pp. 20–52.

GREENBLATT, B. (1977). *Responsibility for Child Care: The Changing Role of Family and State in Child Care.* San Francisco, Calif.: Jossey-Bass.

HOLMAN, R. (1976). *Inequality in Child Care.* Child Poverty Action Group Pamphlet No. 26. London: Child Poverty Action Group.

JOFFE, C. E. (1977). *Friendly Intruders: Childcare Professonals and Family Life.* Berkeley, Calif.: University of California Press.

KAMERMAN, S. B., and KAHN, A. J. (eds.) (1978) *Family Policy: Government and Families in Fourteen Countries.* New York: Columbia University Press.

MORONEY, R. M. (1976). *The Family and the State.* Harlow: Longman.

NATIONAL COUNCIL FOR SOCIAL SERVICE (1979). 'The Family Forum Steering Group Report' (mimeo). London: National Council for Social Service.

PACKMAN, J. (1975). *The Child's Generation: Child Care Policy from Curtis to Houghton.* Oxford: Basil Blackwell/Martin Robertson.

POULTON, G., and CAMPBELL, G. (1979). *Families with Young Children.* (Report of a Hampshire-based study project into co-operative professional care.) Hampshire Area Health Authority and County Council, with the University of Southampton.

RATHBONE, E. F. (1924; 3rd edition 1927). *The Disinherited Family.* London: Allen and Unwin.

WYNN, M. (1970). *Family Policy.* London: Michael Joseph.

YOUNG, M., and WILLMOTT, P. (1973). *The Symmetrical Family.* London: Routledge and Kegan Paul.

# CHAPTER 7

Epilogue

*There are only two lasting things we can leave our children: one is roots, the other is wings.*

Across the world many parents cannot provide adequately for their offspring because of the constraints of material poverty—inadequate food, clothing, housing and extended medical care. In a developed nation such as Britain, deprivation of this kind remains, though only for a tiny minority, yet it is overlaid for the majority by other kinds of deficit, symptomatic of a materialistic, competitive and individualistic society, in which a rhetoric about child care often replaces widespread self-denying action for the sake of children. Much needed initiatives in the education for parenthood field will not of themselves create a caring new society; a renewed moral and spiritual dynamic seems essential for that. What they may achieve, however, is a stronger body of aware child advocates, whose voting leverage may incrementally shift our society from a patchwork of short-term family crisis remedies to sounder policies of long-term preventive support for all families which could forestall many a crisis. Sound and adequate parenting (and its obverse) is cumulative, and is the crucial transmitter of intellectual, spiritual and bodily health. Lloyd de Mause puts it well:

A society's child-rearing practices are . . . the very condition for the transmission of all other cultural elements, and place definite limits on what can be achieved in all other spheres of history.

As our parents shaped us, so we are now endowed with the responsibility of shaping our children's future, and therefore the future of mankind.

But in arguing for educational and other policy measures to support parents and children in their family situations, we cannot ignore the global context, which was briefly alluded to at the start of the present text (page 1). As a society of technologically sophisticated

130

people with a potential access to knowledge unsurpassed before in human history, we have the power to make many things happen and to control our evolutionary destiny to a significant degree. Yet purposeful action is contingent upon the articulation of a sufficient consensus of belief and moral principle, which can guide and motivate our social and political organisation. If we try to make an insular society in which those who choose to produce new people know in advance something of what being adequate parents involves, and are better supported through and rewarded for being the 'special adults' of their babies and children, within various family lifestyles, while simultaneously ignoring the character of the global family, we will indeed be blinkered and short-sighted.

We know that the world has finite resources, and that the Malthusian controls on population growth—famine, pestilence and war—can now be significantly attenuated. The major religions of the world, and in particular Christianity, present in varying degrees patterns for harmonious coexistence. However, their frequent continuing appeal to the emotions somewhat divorced from the intellect and from technological and social reality is, with the growth of educational opportunity worldwide, leading to their collective loss of influence upon human behaviour, which is thus becoming increasingly mechanistic in its underpinning philosophy. And with that loss of influence, the cultural mechanisms for ensuring the inter-generational succession of fundamental moral principles could easily be weakened. Education for family life, locally and worldwide, must never ignore education for humane population control, since the viability of individual families will increasingly depend upon the viability of the world family, and there are only a few decades left to secure the latter without turbulent dislocations.

The ability of communities to recognise their interdependence, and to act compassionately in consequence, may well originate in the experiences of individuals within much smaller units of social organisation (that is, families) during the crucial stages of their emotional, intellectual and social development. It is here that we can first learn that hanging together can prevent us from hanging separately. In our increasingly competitive and materialistic society, if charity does not begin at home it may not be learned elsewhere, and our species could thus fail to recognise that without charity and the capacity for considerate and unpossessive love, man loses both his uniqueness and his dignity.

In the current climate of adult liberation, in which distortions of self-actualising therapeutic experience have tended to become a new western 'religion', self-denying action sometimes seems an unnecessary virtue. Yet the commitments of mums and dads to each other and to their offspring do mean sacrifices. The challenge within the nuclear group is to create warm, accepting and respectful climates in which sacrifice is not perceived as being a form of grudging abasement, but as an energising force to enlarge the individual's sense of worthiness and fulfilment. This paradox of giving, rather than possessing, to find contentment, lies at the heart of the Christian gospel. We see the historical Jesus in touch with life, breaking conventions which inhibit human outreach, pleading with us individually to discard the inessential, and to follow His example, loving others beyond the requirements of the law in order to find ourselves and truly live. In Maslow's pyramid of human needs (Figure 9) there are no limits set for human growth once the self-transcendant stage is reached.

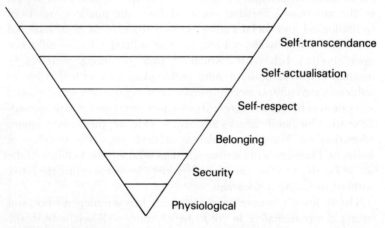

9   *Maslow's pyramid of human needs*

Both the 'family' and 'education' are such elusive symbols and concepts, and may not be summarised for any of us by statistics of gender, income, possessions or performance. Their meaning is worked out for each in particularities, in specific relationships, in specific joys and agonies, and in specific contexts of time and place. Debates about either can often forget, both philosophically and spiritually, the individual hearts which make up collective social sympathies. To deliver a lecture about these topics, and now to write a book about them, is to fall a prey to the same danger. The languages of public argument, of research and of policy-making can so easily seem barren, abstract, shallow and even hypocritical, since they usually lack the warmth, the despair, the richness, the bereavement, and so on, which form the character of the life shaping particulars experienced by each of us. So teachers, authors, social workers, politicians and educational planners may gain insights about the collective realities of our social order through turning to the works of the novelist, poet and playwright and finding in their work reminders of themselves so often concealed within the professional role.

Enthralling stories, such as *War and Peace*, *The Pallisers*, *The Forsyte Saga*, and even *The Archers* and *Coronation Street*, are family dramas. The poetry of the family takes in the warmth or frigidity of intercourse, pains of labour, children's laughter and innocent joy, their terrors and their fears; it includes the tendernesses of courtship, eternal triangles, the violence of husband and of wife seemingly imprisoned in roles they never imagined, let alone predicted; it includes disruption and reconciliation, the hopes and griefs of grandparents, the enhanced records and skills of a new generation tantalisingly demonstrated alongside its failings to grapple with age-old problems; it encompasses the security of home territory, and the pain of accident and loss; it speaks of dreams of success, but also of despair and failure.

The final scene of Eugene O'Neill's *Long Day's Journey Into Night* portrays the family talking on in a declining pool of light and in increasing darkness. Fathers, mothers, sisters, brothers are trying to communicate; understanding but not comprehending; loving each other but hating and hurting too; tangling and untangling like badly-cast fishing lines or like poorly-wound balls of wool, longing to be knit together without loss of stitches for mutual warmth and beauty; a group of at one moment confident, secure, yet at another, wounded, lonely individuals. O'Neill's characters are talking about the family in order to explain their approach towards life itself, reflected as it is in the self-same paradoxes. Perhaps for this reason, the family remains durable in history; it has the continuous potential of genuine, caring intimacy, but seems now destined to require greater variety and flexibility of form.

Thus we can discuss neither families nor indeed the education of their members as if they were like molecules or indigestion. What public information, debate and policy can do is to create external environments which on the one hand do not diminish the potential growth of beings which can take place within homes, and which on the other provide opportunities for people to help each other across and between families through awareness, skill and sensitivity. Our mutual interdependence, and our vulnerability under modern conditions within units which often seem too small, demands more permeable and thus more caring social structures. The Englishman's home is no longer his impregnable castle; it is beseiged from within and without with cries for wider supportive fellowship.

Notwithstanding that the heart of most personal matters rests in particularities rather than statistics, the renewal of interest in the family and its interrelation with educational processes must not retreat to seek private answers to problems of living and being which are collective in nature. And whether we are participating in this movement as parents, teachers, researchers, social workers, medical personnel, or politicians and administrators, our commitments, action and even scholarship must not deny the reality and validity of our individual biographies.

Even for this science-trained author, and somewhat to his surprise, poetry thus becomes the necessary conclusion in order to catch a glimpse of both the Utopia which helped to frame the questions, and the varied experience which suggested at least the first part of the answers.

Education for Parenthood could lead to the transformation of our social structures and the unleashing of our innate capacities to love and care for each other more effectively. That has been the core of concern of this book, and is the single most proper objective for educational and social policy.

## His Family New

Families often are                    conflicting, constricting,
                                      distressing, depressing,
                                      elusive, exclusive,
                                      shakeable, breakable —
Disadvantage for a lifetime.

But families also are                 invigorating, liberating,
                                      alluring, securing,
                                      enrolling, consoling,
                                      tempting, cementing —
Havens in a heartless world.

Jesus born into a family at the first Christmas
Had caring parents, who in anxious consternation
Watched the unfolding of His vocation:
God-made-man, to share our joy and pain,
To identify with our loss and gain,
Demonstrating infinite love, transforming social structures.

No parent He, but friend of all —
Mothers, fathers, children, bachelors, spinsters, to call
To follow Him, self to sacrifice,
To live in open fellowship, then one day, paradise.

                                      Richard C. Whitfield

# The Preparation for Parenthood Group

As the main text has made clear, the activities in Education for Parenthood are scattered and uncoordinated. As a consequence of the diversity of academic and practical disciplines involved, the field is regarded in many quarters as being of low status, and there are still powerful forces within the education service which misguidedly view 'education for living' as a narrow utilitarian concept which is incompatible with the finer goals of 'liberal education'. Recently, moves towards breaking down some of the barriers between the formal school curriculum and the worlds of work and home external to the school have met strong opposition from those teachers who are anxious to preserve professional territory.

When attempts to persuade the Schools Council to allocate resources to support and encourage work in schools in this field proved abortive in 1976, Sir Richard Acland suggested bringing together informally a small group of preventive care enthusiasts to exert some pressure upon central government departments and other relevant bodies. The group includes:

| | |
|---|---|
| *Sir Richard Acland* | (Formerly MP and College of Education Lecturer) |
| *Mrs Dorothy Baldwin* | (Teacher and author of books on child development) |
| *Professor Ronald Davie* | (Professor of Educational Psychology, University College, Cardiff) |
| *Dr Mia Kellmer Pringle* | (Director, National Children's Bureau, London) |
| *Miss Margaret Maden* | (Headmistress, Islington Green School, London) |
| *Professor John Nisbet* | (Professor of Education, University of Aberdeen) |

| | |
|---|---|
| *Professor Jack Tizard** | (Director, Thomas Coram Research Unit, University of London Institute of Education) |
| *Lady Ethel Venables* | (Educational Psychologist; Vice-President of the National Marriage Guidance Council) |
| *Professor Richard Whitfield* | (Correspondent) |

The group has no formal constitution, but formulates its views independently and has been received officially in London at both the Department of Education and Science and the Department of Health and Social Security. The group intends to phase itself out of existence when it feels that there are significant initiatives taking place at the research, development and intervention levels with regard to preparing tomorrow's parents and supporting more adequately those who already have the care of children.

# Some Specific Recent Initiatives in the field of Education for Parenthood

NOTE: There is a wide range of continuing yet uncoordinated development in this and related fields. This select appendix simply indicates a few of the more substantial examples from within the English speaking world.

Gillian Pugh's recent paper *Preparation for Parenthood: Some Current Initiatives and Thinking* (National Children's Bureau, 1980), prepared for a seminar on the subject at the National Children's Bureau, will also be found a helpful complement to this selective listing.

## A     USA

In 1972 the US Federal Office of Education in the Department of Health, Education and Welfare began funding an extensive six year nationwide program called 'Education for Parenthood' (EFP), with a budget of almost £3,000,000. The major purposes of the pump-priming venture were to provide *teenagers* with the opportunities to develop more positive attitudes about children and parenting, to improve their self-awareness and understanding, and to increase their knowledge and skills in the following areas:

(*a*) basic child development;

(*b*) the social, medical and emotional needs of children;

(*c*) the family's role in child development and socialisation;

(*d*) prenatal care and the early months of infancy;

(*e*) child care career possibilities and requirements.

Since its inception, EFP has focussed national attention on the need for adolescents to have formal instruction and actual experience in working with young children so as to answer their questions about children and parenthood, to improve their competence as prospective parents, and to prepare them for possible careers in working with children.

The EFP structured curriculum materials have been used in many secondary high schools, colleges, universities and community agencies. A central unit in EFP is a one-year elective course 'Exploring Childhood' for use with thirteen to eighteen-year-old boys and girls of varied backgrounds. A prime concern of this course, which deliberately omits sex education, is to create a climate in which students feel relaxed about discussing such personal topics as experiences they have had with small children, their own expectations of youngsters and their own memories of childhood. Child development theory is interwoven with field experiences in a context which avoids an approach based upon a single correct way of dealing with children. Through the course, increased understanding of the self and others has been reported, leading to improved family relationships for students: for example, greater tolerance of younger siblings and better communication with parents. One mother reported the change in her son's attitude to school:

'I used to have to almost kick him out of bed to get him off to school, but now he's on the first shift of the day care centre he is up early and so enthusiastic about those little kids . . . and he's doing much better in all his other classes too.'

(See further: Ogg, E., 'Preparing Tomorrow's Parents', Public Affairs Pamphlet No. 520, New York, 1975; a series of these pamphlets covers a range of issues in family life.)

In addition, an important part of EFP involved seven national voluntary youth-serving agencies (including the Salvation Army and the Boy/Girl Scouts) which were awarded three-year grants to conduct a variety of pilot projects for teenagers in non-school settings. The voluntary organisations have developed a range of innovative ways of providing teenagers from a wide variety of economic and cultural backgrounds with information and experience about child development and family life through working in the homes of pre-schoolers, in child care centres, day camps and hospitals, and with handicapped children. Comments of two teenage participants were:

'Before I thought I'd get married right away and have children. Now I want to wait until I'm mature enough to be a good parent.'
'I had not thought of a career in working with children before. This program made me aware that having children yourself is not the only way of having a close association with children.'

Independent evaluation has been an integral part of EFP activities and a range of significant gains in teenagers' knowledge skills and sensitivities has been reported (Morris, L.A. (ed.), *Education for Parenthood: A Program, Curriculum and Evaluation Guide,* US Department of Health, Education and Welfare, 1977.) Many other US programs relating to EFP are available through Federal, State or more local initiatives, but the picture is one of lack of coordination and adequate evaluation. In addition, long-term preventive care policies are not fashionable, and existing innovations reach a minority of those in need. Hence, despite far greater investment in innovation compared with the UK, policy impacts are little different for the majority.

## B    SOME UK LOCAL EDUCATION AUTHORITY SCHEMES

### Gloucestershire

This county pioneered one of the first LEA schemes entitled 'Education in Personal Relationships and Family Life' which was originally conceived in 1962 under the impetus of the Gloucestershire Association for Family Life. This Association, which included representatives of a wide range of voluntary and statutory organisations, was concerned to promote its objectives in both educational circles and the wider community. The third edition of the scheme's handbook was published in 1971 and its influence is still present within the schools, the youth and further education services, though no research-based reports into its effectiveness have been published. The scheme has however undoubtedly influenced developments elsewhere.

### City of Birmingham

In 1975–6 two conferences took place in Birmingham which acted as a catalyst for strengthening work in this field in the City's schools. Now a CSE internally assessed (mode 3) examination is offered within a framework of total curriculum options by 15 schools in 'Child Development and the Family' with the following eight common core section syllabus:

the family; adolescence; preparation for parenthood; growth and development of the foetus; the child's emotional, social, mental and physical development from birth to five years; safety of the child and family; children with special needs; the child and his school.

In addition, one option is taken from: (*i*) needlecraft/fabrics for children; (ii) food education; (iii) play and toys; (iv) music, art and drama related to child development; and (v) language and illustrated stories for young children.

Assessment is by written and oral examination; coursework and a child study project diary is also considered. A teachers' booklet, *Child Development Courses in Secondary Schools* (1977), is also available. Approaching 2000 CSE candidates from the City are now involved each year using both mode 1 and mode 3 forms of presentation: this is about 10% of the City's total year group. Of the candidates, 99.8% are girls, but the lack of interest among boys has not been reflected in Home Economics courses where there has been a steady increase over recent years.

### Inner London

The ILEA has work in progress in child development and family studies in many of its schools, usually based in Home Economics Departments. Following the pattern elsewhere, girls vastly predominate in the classes in which serious study takes place. A working party containing advisory teachers continues to prepare curriculum guidelines (including reference to syllabus overlap with related fields) and support materials for the 'Child Development and the Family' course which aims:

   (a)  to encourage a greater awareness of the needs of young children through learning about environmental and other circumstances which may affect their development; and

   (b)  to help students to come to a better self-understanding and become caring and responsible adults and parents in the future.

(See *Resources for Child Development and the Family Courses*, ILEA, 1979.)

The syllabus, leading to the CSE award of the Metropolitan Regional Examinations Board, includes:

   family and kinship; marriage and parenthood; growth and development from conception; family adjustment to the new baby; physical and emotional needs of baby and young child; communication and language development; stimulating environment; personality development; social training; sick and handicapped children; safety and first aid; adoption, fostering, one parent families, neglected children and those in care. Practical experience with children is central to the course, and is provided by playgroups, day nurseries, one o'clock clubs, nursery schools and reception classes.

Over 2,000 candidates presented themselves for CSE assessment in this course in 1978.

*Norfolk*

In this county, the Education Department has recently collaborated with the Area Health Authority to produce a secondary school 'Health and Social Education' programme which lists the following core content topics 'in which it would be desirable to involve as many pupils as possible as a preparation for living'.

*Physical Health*:

personal hygiene, communicable diseases, risk factors in preventable disease, first aid, human biology

*Mental and Emotional Health*:

feelings and emotional and developmental needs of adults and children, relationships and marriage

*Social and Community Health*:

environmental health, home-making, the mass media, health and social services, world health

For the eleven to fourteen age range, the county working party recommend that appropriate topics, and more particularly factual information, should be taught through existing subjects, such as science, and religious and physical education. For the fourteen to sixteen range, about one hour per week is suggested for a separate programme of studies over two years.

NOTE: Significant work is also in progress in many other LEAs, such as Lancashire, Bedfordshire, Devon, Waltham Forest and Coventry. It is expected that some kind of national descriptive summary will emanate from the DES funded project referred to in Appendix 3 (page 154). Here the intention has simply been to be illustrative.

C    SCHOOLS COUNCIL HEALTH EDUCATION PROJECTS

Although there has not yet been a national curriculum development project in the Education for Parenthood field specifically, in the mid 1970s two projects in Health Education have been funded chiefly by the Schools Council and intended respectively for the five to thirteen and thirteen to eighteen age ranges. In these projects, Health Education is seen chiefly as a part of the broad process of socialisation with emphasis being placed on helping youngsters to make informed choices in matters related to their total health. As such, the curriculum units are concerned with the development of positive pupil self-images and attitudes, and with decision-making skills, as well as with providing the relevant knowledge from medicine and the social sciences. While not ruling out specific timetabling for health education in schools and colleges, the projects see much of the necessary work being done through a range of other relevant subjects, but with adequate institutional coordination. One function of the projects has been to gather together many of the diverse resource materials, and parts of the output of both projects are relevant to the preparation for parenthood field. Indeed, one of the eight main content areas currently featured in the thirteen to eighteen project is entitled 'Education for Parenthood', with examples of study items being the growth of young children, family roles and structures, and helping youngsters cope with loss and separation.

D    TWO EXAMPLES FROM EXAMINATION BODIES

*Southern Regional Examinations Board: CSE in Parentcraft*
The following syllabus (reproduced here by the kind permission of the Board) is a model of concise language, guidelines and layout. The course is being taken by sixteen-year-olds entering for the Certificate of Secondary Education in the Board's region. Around 160 hours of teaching contact time are suggested, that is roughly 10% of the available formal curriculum time during the last two years of compulsory schooling. In 1979, around 2,500 candidates were entered for assessment by schools, chiefly by the external mode I, and the popularity of the course has doubled since 1976.

*Syllabus and assessment scheme (1980 edition)*
*Aims*
    The aims of this course of studies are as follows:
 (1)  To prepare students of both sexes for aspects of family life.
 (2)  To encourage them to be aware of and to be sympathetic to the responsibilities which come with marriage, the birth of children and the establishment of a family unit.
 (3)  To realise the value of a happy, healthy and stable family background in the physical, mental and moral development of the individual.

*Objectives*

The course not only has these overall aims in mind, but the candidates are expected to achieve the following educational objectives which the elements of the course are designed to assess:

(1) A knowledge of the anatomy and physiology of the human body in relation to
   (a) the development of both partners through adolescence to adulthood,
   (b) the process of procreation and
   (c) child development and growth.

(2) A knowledge of and an ability to evaluate the importance of the rules of health.

(3) A knowledge of the causes of accidents in the home, methods of prevention and the practical ability to deal with them.

(4) Practical ability in craft-work to enable the child to produce equipment for the nursery, and also toys and garments.

(5) A knowledge of the stages of a child's intellectual development and the modes of learning appropriate to each stage.

(6) A knowledge of the psychological development of the child and the ability to select the appropriate solution for behavioural problems in the context of family life.

(7) An understanding of the contribution which an inadequate family life can make towards social problems, e.g. drug-taking, delinquency.

(8) A knowledge of the tensions created by the interaction of personalities within a family, their possible consequences and the contribution which the supportive services can make.

(9) A knowledge of decisions which might have to be made leading up to marriage, in marriage and in family life, e.g. the choice of a partner, size of family, division of responsibilities, etc., and an ability to establish priorities in decision-making.

(10) The ability to evaluate the moral and social issues basic to the existence of a family (e.g. the sanctity of life, population explosion, etc.).

*Facilities*

(1) It is felt that this course will be best handled by an Integrated Studies team of staff in which Home Economics, Science and Humanities departments would play a major part or, alternatively, interrelated contributions from all three areas. In

either case it is important that overall direction is given to ensure the balance of the course.

(2) Attention is drawn to resources available to schools through local Health Departments and to the availability of qualified staff working in a number of associated areas, who are often prepared to help.

(3) In order to give full scope to the practical objectives of the course, visits and work experience in clinics, nurseries, day nurseries, pre-school playgroups and local infant schools should be explored to the full.

(4) It is suggested that an appropriate time allocation for this course would be 4 periods a week over 2 years.

(5) The following is intended as a guide to achieving the objectives listed. The extent to which staff develop each section will depend on individual circumstances. Numbers listed at each section heading refer to the appropriate objectives. This should not be regarded as exclusive.

SECTION 1  *Preparation for Marriage*          (objectives 1(*a*); 9; 10)
1 Simple anatomy and physiology.
2 General health—V.D., drugs, smoking, etc.—effects on health.
3 The Engagement—choosing a partner—hereditary diseases, etc.
4 Marriage—meaning, preparation, etc., the ceremony.

SECTION 2  *The Family*      (objectives 1(*b*); (*c*); 2; 7; 8; 9; 10)
5 Contraception—various methods. Objections—disadvantages.
6 Conception.
7 Normal pregnancy—pre-natal health.
8 Arrangements for delivery.
9 Birth.
10 Father's rôle during pregnancy and birth.

SECTION 3  *Caring for the Child*          (objectives 1(*c*); 2; 3; 4)
11 Layette, equipment and the nursery.
12 Safety measures.
13 Hygiene of the child's environment.
14 Personal hygiene of the child.

15 Normal stages of physical development.

16 Infant feeding, e.g. breast feeding; artificial feeding; weaning.

17 Basic dietic requirements.

18 Minor accidents and first aid.

19 Minor ailments.

20 Symptoms and signs of common infectious diseases.

21 Supportive services for the family.

SECTION 4   *The Child Growing Up*                    (objectives 3; 5; 6; 8)

22 The behaviour of the new born child.

23 Norms of spontaneous development, e.g. sight; hearing; touch; sitting; walking.

24 Individual differences in the stages of physical development of children.

25 Emotional development of the child and how care and environment affect this by association with adults; other children; dependence; independence; discipline and self control; family relationships; common causes of children's behavioural difficulties.

SECTION 5   *The Child Learning*                         (objectives 5; 6)

26 Learning at home. The supreme importance of the good mother; some common defects at home; the only child; adult environment; erratic and harsh discipline, the slum.

27 The value of the nursery and nursery school.

28 Simple guidance on the main training problems relating to

(a) Play: freedom to play and to let others play; child's care of toys; use of educative apparatus; use of organised play activities; physical, imaginative manipulative play; co-operative play.

(b) Speech: importance of example; common impediments.

(c) Use of specific educative 'material'—sand, clay, plasticine, dough, water, etc.

(d) Nursery rhymes: origin and significance; basic requirements.

(e) Music and basic movement: rhythm, percussion, songs and games; organisation of a typical 'session'.

(f) Make-believe: story telling; dramatics.

    (g) Books: stories and poetry; 'good' literature; pleasing art.

    (h) Art: drawing and painting techniques; tearing, cutting, pasting, mounting.

    (i) Conduct of meals and birthday parties, Hallowe'en and Christmas parties. Tables; decorations; games planning; picnics.

29 The outdoors: the nature table; care of pets; responsibility to animals.

*Assessment*

Assessment of the objectives is to be by the following methods:

(1) Theory paper — to be issued by the Board.

(2) Oral — to be by means of an oral test to be issued on the day of the written examination.

(3) Practicals — a practical test for periodic assessment, issued by the Board to test (i) dietetics and (ii) the care of the young child.

(4) Craft work — craft work produced during the course to be assessed at local consortium moderation.

(5) Folder — to be the student's record of child development as seen in visits.

(6) Observation — unobtrusive assessment by observation of the candidate in the course of visits.

(7) Discussion — teacher assessment of the candidate in 'discussion' situation.

Note: For assessments (2), (4), (5), (6) and (7) information regarding the criteria of assessment are issued by the Board to schools.

The grid on page 148 links the methods of assessment to the objectives. It also gives the weightings for each of the objectives and for each of the methods of assessment.

| Objectives | Theory | | Discussion | Practical | Practice | | | Weighting of Objective |
| | Written Paper | Oral | | | Folder | Assessment by Observation | |
|---|---|---|---|---|---|---|---|
| 1 | 7 | 3 | | | | | 10 |
| 2 | 5 | | | 10 | | | 15 |
| 3 | 5 | 3 | | | | | 8 |
| 4 | | | | 10 | | | 10 |
| 5 | 2 | 3 | | | 5 | 2½ | 12½ |
| 6 | | | 4 | | 5 | 2½ | 11½ |
| 7 | 5 | | 4 | | | | 9 |
| 8 | 6 | | 4 | | | | 10 |
| 9 | | 3 | 4 | | | | 7 |
| 10 | | 3 | 4 | | | | 7 |
| | 30 | 15 | 20 | 20 | 10 | 5 | 100 |
| | 45% | | 20% | | 35% | | |

*National Association for Maternal and Child Welfare*

This voluntary organisation (NAMCW) provides a progressive series of courses in the care of children and human development leading to certification by the Association, which can also accrue credit for the Duke of Edinburgh Award schemes. Although the courses may be taught in schools, other contexts such as youth clubs and evening classes for adults are envisaged.

The aims of the basic and general courses are:

To contribute towards the education of young people for personal relationships, family life, parenthood and citizenship by:

(*i*) creating awareness of emotional, intellectual, social, spiritual and physical needs particularly those of children, and providing guidelines for the fulfilment of these;

(*ii*) clarifying ideas already absorbed at home and affording opportunities to discuss differing family and cultural patterns;

(*iii*) helping the rising generation to consider seriously the contribution they may make to society in the future.

NAMCW believes that a great deal of self-knowledge and understanding can be achieved through the study of child care and child development. In standards of behaviour and reflections on personal behaviour and in discussing any need for disciplining children, the benefit of self-discipline may be considered. There should arise some insight into other people's points of view—parents, relatives, the elderly, teachers, those in authority generally, and relationships between the sexes may be seen in a fresh light.

For more advanced work there is an additional aim of providing a flexible training course for students who wish to work with children or families.

Students are expected to learn how to assess and attempt to meet the needs of children. They should become able to look after other people's children competently and learn how to cope in emergencies. Also they should be able to assist in a team where knowledge and a sense of responsibility are imperative.

No specific contact time is stipulated for the basic course, save for a *minimum* of about 50 hours, i.e. one double period per week throughout a school year. Assessment is by written and oral tests, and practical work with children during the course is expected. The two more advanced courses provided by the Association naturally demand a greater study time and practical experience, and the assessment requirements are correspondingly more demanding. The total number of candidates for the NAMCW examinations has doubled during the 1970s and now stands at about 7000 per year.

Syllabuses are available from NAMCW at 1 South Audley Street, London, W1Y 6JS, which also publishes a useful practical booklet for teachers, *Parentcraft Education* compiled by Leonora Pitcairn, and *Parentcraft Education Teaching Aids* (1978).

E    TELEVISION AND RADIO INITIATIVES

Over the years, television and radio have increasingly been seen as a stimulus to social action. Viewers and listeners have been actively encouraged to respond to programmes by offering their services as volunteers, or to ask for some kind of assistance. The telephone, too, has played its part, as an instrument of immediate communication and response, which can marshal resources on a large scale and across the UK.

Both the BBC and the Independent Broadcasting Authority have longstanding commitments to provide practical help through television on aspects of child-rearing and family life. Recent programmes,

excluding those intended for helping physically and mentally handicapped children, or non-English speakers, are now briefly listed.

## Mum's the Word (ITV)

A six-programme series broadcast in 1974 and 1975 with particular
emphasis on the role of parents in encouraging language development
among their pre-school children.

## Starting Out (ITV)

A ten-programme series (third version 1979) about relationships.
Social, moral and practical questions are raised in a manner appealing
to adolescents; teachers' notes are available.

## Facts for Life: Family Matters (ITV)

The first four programmes are concerned with approximately the two-
year period from conception. Factual information on pregnancy, birth
and post-natal care is conveyed in the context of the experience, for
both mothers and fathers, of becoming parents. The second four
programmes cover some important aspects of the early years of
parenthood in order to give some idea of what it feels like to become
responsible for the care and development of a growing baby. The series
is being used in schools.

## All about Babies (ITV)

A thirteen-programme series in magazine format dating from 1977
and covering approximately the first two years of life with most stress
on pregnancy, birth and early baby care.

## All about Toddlers (ITV)

This complementary series of ten programmes transmitted from 1979
deals with child care from six months to five years, again in magazine
format and designed to appeal to adults with the minimum of formal
education. Topics covered include: crying babies, immunization,
parental anxieties, child sickness, sources of help, growth and development, play, working mothers.

## Other People's Children (BBC TV Childminders' Project)

A nineteen-programme series, also dating from 1977, designed to raise
the morale and competence of childminders who care for the under-
fives whose parents go out to work; also intended to help social workers
and others involved in the training of childminders, many of whom are
unregistered. A handbook accompanies the series.

### It's a Great Life, if You Don't Weaken (BBC TV)

This is a two-phase series of about twenty programmes, dating from April 1979, and aimed at parents of children of any age, from birth to eighteen. Having a magazine format and a minimal input of 'expert' advice, the series aims to increase parental morale through the use of humour and to help parents appreciate that there is no one right way to rear children. The series is associated with a 'phone-in referral network of family advice centres set up by the National Children's Home using volunteers ('Family Network'), and a BBC-published companion book about relationships is available. This series is being independently evaluated (see Appendix 3).

### Child Abuse (BBC TV)

A series of five programmes planned for 1980 and designed to introduce the latest thinking about the social pathology of child abuse to members of the caring professions, to families at risk, and to the general public.

### Parents and Children (BBC TV)

A longstanding series dating from 1973, and now comprising sixty programmes, it originally sought to keep parents informed of developments in the fields of education, health and the law. Later emphases have been towards providing parents with insights into children's physical, emotional and educational development to assist them in their role in the family setting within modern society.

### The First Years of Life (Open University with BBC TV and Radio)

An eight-week non-degree course for parents produced in association with the Health Education Council, which takes parents and parents-to-be from the act of conception through pregnancy up to the child's age of two. The course answers questions, deals with problems and shows parents how to help the young child grow and learn. Support books and records are available which present the material in an attractive non-prescriptive manner which appeals to a wide range of intellectual abilities.

### The Pre-school Child (Open University with BBC TV and Radio)

Also an eight-week course, not eligible for degree credit, and produced in association with the Pre-school Playgroups Association. The approach is practical rather than theoretical, and there are lively back-up records and print materials, all designed to help parents keep their two to five-year-olds busy, happy and learning, without becoming anxious about the tasks.

(Formal participation in each of these two Open University courses currently costs £10 per course and initial enrolments were 96% female with 84% being under the age of 36. With the aid of a grant from the Health Education Council, the course materials are to be adapted for use in schools.)

## Childhood 5 to 10 (Open University/BBC)

This eight-week course starting October 1979 follows on from 'The Pre-school Child' and aims to help parents contribute to the personal, social and intellectual development of their five to ten year-old children through the appropriate management of the physical and emotional environment. It encourages parents to identify and create opportunities for their children and to support their development towards independence. Parent/parent and parent/child relationships are examined, as is the child's own developing attitudes towards parenthood.

## Parent Education Programming on Independent Local Radio

Guidance to parents on aspects of bringing up children is generally covered in two programming styles on independent local radio. The first is a regular time or series devoted to parent education. The second consists of insertions into magazine programmes; these may not be very regular nor very long. Virtually all features, however, are done with the help and guidance of local experts or organisations.

Some ten local radio stations are involved in regular programming of events in this field on topics which have covered health education, including immunisation, safety at home and on the roads, children's books and play, pre-school playgroups, teenage problems and fostering. About eight stations are currently involved with occasional features. 'Phone-in facilities for both on-air questions and answers and off-air advice have been provided in many cases.

## BBC Radio

There have been several BBC radio series over recent years of interest to parents on topics such as reading, children's books, school and community, teaching music, and trends in the educational system. Perhaps the most interesting innovation relevant to childrearing has been 'Child Care Switchboard', a 1977 experiment involving six BBC local radio stations which had associated public and private 'phone-in facilities. A total of 24 hours of live broadcasting time was made available with 103 hours of private line listening. Blocked telephone lines presented a problem in estimating demand, but over 500 callers were logged regarding childcare problems, in some cases needing urgent assistance. A report of the experiment has been prepared by the National Educational Research and Development Trust and contains a number of reflective pointers for the future use of radio in this field.

# Related Work at the University of Aston Department of Educational Enquiry

In July 1978 and January 1979 two research contracts in the 'education and family life' field were awarded to the University of Aston in Birmingham's Department of Educational Enquiry under the author's direction. Unlike the majority of University Departments of Education, the Aston Department is not formally involved in pre-service teacher training (save through 'sandwich' provision with another institution) and has traditions in the fields of counselling and human communication, in addition to educational studies. Whilst the bases and practice of formal educational provision in schools and colleges are of fundamental interest to the Department, contexts of teaching and learning in the home, the community, at work and through the media are also considered to be crucial, as is their inter-relation with the more formal educational and supporting agencies. The two policy-oriented research projects are therefore compatible with this ethos and brief details of them are given below.

## A PREPARATION FOR PARENTHOOD IN THE SECONDARY SCHOOL CURRICULUM

Sponsor: Department of Education and Science
Duration: Three years from July 1979

The chief aim of this research is to make an assessment of the objectives, timetable structures, teaching approaches, and outcomes of secondary school curriculum units designed to provide some preparation for pupils for their possible later responsibilities as parents.

### Fieldwork

This is to be executed in about five local authority areas, having different demographic compositions, in which educationally significant and interesting work in the preparation for parenthood field has been taking place for some time. The history of the development of these local initiatives will be charted, including reference to personnel, intentions, syllabus construction, curriculum materials, resources, pupil access, uptake and assessment.

Through this case study approach, which will include work in schools and the communities which they serve, it is planned to develop a map of curriculum aims and content based upon the views expressed by teachers, social workers, community workers, medical personnel and parents. The work observed in schools will then be evaluated with respect to these views and more recent central government proposals, taking into account the constraints experienced by the teachers involved.

Pupil attitudes, skills, and knowledge acquired through the course units provided will be surveyed to assess the feasibility of preparing young people for family responsibility prior to leaving school. As appropriate, external measures of pupils' aptitudes, either individually or collectively, will also be taken: for example, the views of parents, peers, teachers or other professionals within the urban, suburban and rural contexts of study. These enquiries will assist in defining the nature of the need as well as shedding light upon how and whether it is being met.

It is anticipated that much of the work in schools will involve the research team in collaborating with teachers of home economics, human biology, religious, moral and health education. Objectives concerned with education in personal and social relationships will also be included for analysis. Although of no less importance, it is unlikely to be possible to concentrate much attention on the particular issues confronting ethnic minorities in this context.

It is hoped that the project's reports will enable policy guidelines to be framed at the school, local and national levels.

B    EVALUATION OF A NEW BBC TELEVISION SERIES OF PROGRAMMES ON FAMILY LIFE AND THE PROBLEMS OF PARENTHOOD

Sponsor:      Health Education Council
Duration:     Two years from January 1979 (fieldwork at BBC commenced October 1978)

*Purpose*
The primary aim of this project concerns the evaluation of the making

and impacts of viewing of a new series of programmes on family and parent issues, launched in the spring of 1979 by the Further Education Department of BBC Television, and entitled 'It's a Great Life, if You Don't Weaken' (see also page 150).

The history and the continuing developmental and production processes of the series are being observed and analysed. The impact of the transmitted programmes and their effects upon various groupings of audiences is being assessed in terms of action, attitudes, and problem-solving, and in relation to the intentions of the programme-makers. A significant part of the audience is those viewers who, as a result of watching the programmes, turn to the featured statutory and voluntary agencies for advice and guidance with personal family problems. A further sphere of attention concerns audience reaction to written support material accompanying the programmes.

*The nature of the innovation being evaluated*
The new series of programmes draw on the BBC's considerable past experience and expertise in helping parents to understand, contribute to, and participate in the development of their children. The programmes are, however, innovative on two counts: first, in respect of their magazine format and their presentation; and secondly, because as well as experts, families drawn from the programme's audience participate in the making of the series, with viewers being encouraged to make their opinions and ideas for the programmes known. In this sense, the programmes, which also refer to topical events and present news of concern to families, are properly described as 'interactive'.

The television series, in covering the skills and understandings pertinent to parenthood and family life, necessarily features numerous organisations. In addition, they are specifically linked to the telephone advice service set up at Family Network Centres newly opened by the National Children's Home (NCH). While the NCH has established its centres independently of the BBC series, they are linked with the television programmes as one agency to contact initially, should further advice be required. The centres are chiefly staffed by volunteers, who may be able to undertake the necessary counselling or practical help themselves, or who otherwise will know of or find out who else can help out in the given circumstances.

The innovative aspect of the centres for the NCH is that they represent a further step in working with families as a whole. They are therefore part of the move nationally, in both statutory and voluntary agencies, away from providing separate residential establishments for children whose parents are not able to care for them, towards a policy of working jointly with children and their parents in a mutually familiar and supportive setting: for example, in their own home, or in local neighbourhood centres attended during the day and evening.

Following usual BBC practice, a book was commissioned to accompany the television series, (*It's a Great Life* by Dorothy Baldwin, 1979); published by the BBC, the NCH helps to ensure that it receives a wide distribution.

### Fieldwork

The evaluation requires systematic study of the relevant decision-making processes and their outcomes in both the BBC and the NCH, in order to set the development of the television programmes and of the Family Network Centres in their context and environment. It is also essential to determine the respective intentions of both service providers. Such study is being directed at the history, structure and management execution of each initiative, as well as at its continuing progress.

In terms of the impact of the television programmes upon their audience, several groupings of viewers have been identified and are being followed up within the constraints of research methodology and resources. A range of research techniques are being used in order to make the study as sensitive as possible to the complexities of the innovations.

### Output

It is expected that the research project's evidence will feed into the development of future broadcasting, educational, and social policy initiatives, including further collaboration between voluntary and public welfare agencies and the media.

# Select Bibliography

ARMYTAGE, W. H. G., and PEEL, J. (eds.) (1978). *Perimeters of Social Repair.* London: The Eugenics Society/Academic Press.

BARRITT, G. E. (ed.) (1979). *Family Life: 1978 Conference Papers.* (Occasional Paper No. 1). London: National Children's Home.

BELL, R. Q., and HARPER, L. V. (1977). *Child Effects on Adults.* New York and Chichester: Lawrence Erlbaum/John Wiley.

BERRY, J. (1972). *Social Work with Children.* London: Routledge and Kegan Paul.

BOWLBY, J. (1953). *Child Care and the Growth of Love.* Harmondsworth: Penguin Books.

BRIM, O. G. (1959). *Education for Child Rearing.* New York: Russell Sage.

CENTRAL ADVISORY COUNCIL FOR EDUCATION (1967). *Children and their Primary Schools.* (The Plowden Report). London: HMSO.

COMMITTEE ON CHILD HEALTH SERVICES (1976). *Fit for the Future.* (The Court Report), Vols 1 and 2. London: HMSO.

CLARKE-STEWART, A. (1977). *Child Care in the Family.* New York: Academic Press.

FITZHERBERT, K. (1977). *Child Care Services and the Teacher.* London: Temple Smith.

FYSON, N. L. and GREENHILL, S. (1979). *Family Life.* London: Macmillan.

KELLMER PRINGLE, M. L. (1975). *The Needs of Children.* London: Hutchinson.

KELLMER PRINGLE, M. L. (1980). *A Fairer Future for Children: Towards Better Parental and Professional Care.* London: Macmillan.

KELLMER PRINGLE, M. L., and NAIDOO, S. (1975). *Early Child Care in Britain.* London: Gordon and Breach.

KENNISTON, K. and the CARNEGIE COUNCIL ON CHILDREN (1977). *All Our Children: The American Family under Pressure.* New York: Harcourt Brace Jovanovich.

LASCH, C. (1977). *Haven in a Heartless World*. New York: Basic Books.

LEACH, P. (1979). *Who Cares?* Harmondsworth: Penguin Books.

MASLOW, A. H. (1970). *Motivation and Personality*. New York: Harper and Row.

MIDDLETON, N. (1971). *When Family Failed: The Treatment of Children in the Care of the Community in the First Half of the Twentieth Century*. London: Gollancz.

O'NEILL, O., and RUDDICK, W. (eds.) (1980). *Having Children: Philosophical and Legal Reflections on Parenthood*. Oxford: Oxford University Press.

PILLING, D., and KELLMER PRINGLE, M. L. (1978). *Controversial Issues in Child Development*. London: Elek.

RAPOPORT, R., RAPOPORT, R. N., and STRELITZ, Z. (1977). *Fathers, Mothers and Others*. London: Routledge and Kegan Paul.

RUTTER, M. (1972). *Maternal Deprivation Reassessed*. Harmondsworth: Penguin Books.

RUTTER, M. and MADGE, N. (1976). *Cycles of Disadvantage*. London: Heinemann.

RUTTER, M., TIZARD, J., and WHITMORE, K. (1970). *Education, Health and Behaviour*. Harlow: Longman.

TIZARD, J., MOSS, P., and PERRY, J. (1976). *All Our Children: Pre-school Services in a Changing Society*. London: Temple Smith/New Society.

WINNICOTT, D. W. (1964). *The Child, the Family and the Outside World*. Harmondsworth: Penguin Books.

WILSON, H., and HERBERT, G. W. (1978). *Parents and Children in the Inner City*. London: Routledge and Kegan Paul.

# Index